Escape from Capitalism

CLARA E. MATTEI

Escape from Capitalism
*Economics is Political, and
Other Liberating Truths*

ALLEN LANE
an imprint of
PENGUIN BOOKS

ALLEN LANE

UK | USA | Canada | Ireland | Australia
India | New Zealand | South Africa

Allen Lane is part of the Penguin Random House group of companies whose addresses can be found at global.penguinrandomhouse.com

Penguin Random House UK
One Embassy Gardens, 8 Viaduct Gardens, London SW11 7BW

penguin.co.uk

First published in the USA by Simon and Schuster 2026
First published in Great Britain by Allen Lane 2026
002

Copyright © Clara E. Mattei, 2026

The moral right of the author has been asserted

Penguin Random House values and supports copyright. Copyright fuels creativity, encourages diverse voices, promotes freedom of expression and supports a vibrant culture. Thank you for purchasing an authorized edition of this book and for respecting intellectual property laws by not reproducing, scanning or distributing any part of it by any means without permission. You are supporting authors and enabling Penguin Random House to continue to publish books for everyone.
No part of this book may be used or reproduced in any manner for the purpose of training artificial intelligence technologies or systems. In accordance with Article 4(3) of the DSM Directive 2019/790, Penguin Random House expressly reserves this work from the text and data mining exception.

Printed and bound in Great Britain by Clays Ltd, Elcograf S.p.A.

The authorized representative in the EEA is Penguin Random House Ireland, Morrison Chambers, 32 Nassau Street, Dublin D02 YH68

A CIP catalogue record for this book is available from the British Library

ISBN: 978-0-241-74218-1

Penguin Random House is committed to a sustainable future for our business, our readers and our planet. This book is made from Forest Stewardship Council® certified paper.

*To Galileo, whose laughs and endless "whys"
keep my heart full*

CONTENTS

Introduction: Economics Is a Political Act   1

1. The Invisible Order   19
2. The Logic of Austerity   57
3. The Cruel Math of Unemployment   93
4. The West over the Rest   113
5. Democracy Is Anti-Capitalism   139

    Acknowledgments   165
    Notes   167
    Index   203

Introduction

ECONOMICS IS A POLITICAL ACT

It's the autumn of 1920 and we are in Brussels. Politicians and economists from across Europe sit at worktables, gathered for the first international economic conference in history. Despite the formal tones and elegant attire, the tension in the air is palpable. Their statements form a united, if anguished, front against what they consider an unacceptable disorder, a social chaos that is pushing the capitalist economy to the edge of the abyss.

"The manual workers," declares the English financier Robert H. Brand, "were encouraged to expect, and do expect, some new way of life, some great betterment of their lot. These changes, they believe, at any rate in my country, can be achieved if the system of private industry is replaced by some sort of Government or common ownership. They do not realise the hard truth that . . . a better life can, owing to the losses of the war, be now reached only through labour and suffering."

The conference was organized by the newly created League of Nations in the immediate wake of World War I with a crucial objective: to rebuild an economic order that had collapsed. Across Europe, nations were facing record inflation, food shortages, and mass strikes. Ordinary workers who had suffered during the war were now challenging the monied elite and demanding a complete overhaul of the economic system.

Amid the turmoil of that convulsive moment, politicians and economists fervently advocated a "hard truth": citizens' behavior had to be shaped and controlled according to the principles of economic science. People had to work harder, consume less, and expect little or nothing from the government. It was essential for citizens to renounce any form of labor action or assertion of their economic rights that hindered the flow of capitalist production. Lord Robert Chalmers, former permanent secretary to the British Treasury and one of the representatives of the English delegation, stated it plainly: "Work hard, live hard, save hard."

This motto translated into clear policies: cuts to government budgets, primarily those that funded social services like health insurance and unemployment benefits, along with wage cuts and higher taxes on basic goods.

As they constructed this hard policy package of painful austerity, the technocrats gathered in Brussels were well aware that their plan was far from popular. Inducing citizens to bend to the scientific economic order was easier said than done. The Italian delegate Alberto Beneduce, a professor of economic statistics, had no doubts about the tactic to use: it was necessary to "act on public opinion, on the psychological state of the masses, so that they would no more *impede* but help to re-establish the budget of the state." Beneduce voiced these concerns during the plenary discussion on September 20, 1920.

The date is significant. In those days and weeks in Italy, class struggle had reached its peak. Factory occupations were spreading like wildfire. Throughout the Italian peninsula, for over a month, workers in more than sixty cities had taken direct control of production in all sectors, from mines to dockyards, railways to textile factories. The newspaper of the establishment, the *Corriere della sera*, captured the vibrant beginnings of the occupation in Milan: "The factories yesterday evening presented a singular spectacle. One reached them through crowds of women and children, coming and going with dinners for strikers. . . . Entrances were strictly guarded by groups of workers. Not the ghost of an official or a police officer in sight. The strikers were complete masters of the field." An emblematic photograph taken in September immortalizes this moment of labor empowerment. A group of workers of the factory council—the organ of workers' self-governance—are seated at the desk of Giovanni Agnelli, owner of Fiat, the greatest automobile company in Italy. In the Italian countryside, peasants had taken control of agricultural land and begun managing it with democratic assemblies.

The "psychological state of the masses" leaned into a post-capitalist society in which private ownership of the means of production and power relations between employers and employees would be replaced by a fairer structure. The deadly shock of the Great War had unleashed a new awareness of the simple fact that workers were central to the production of value and wealth. Led by Antonio Gramsci and other labor organizers and intellectuals, the factory councils were new institutions embodying the aspiration of democratic participation in production and distribution. Their efforts were empowering people to consciously exercise economic and political freedom in the "new society of free and equal producers."

Mounting inflation fueled the flames of discontent. As food prices soared, workers called out the private investors profiting from their misery and even began questioning the justice of an economy that was working for only very few. The experts knew that monetary instability was not purely an economic puzzle for economic science to solve. It was inherently a political problem. Revered British economist John Maynard Keynes candidly acknowledged the challenge posed to the existing system: "A continuance of inflationism and high prices will not only depress the exchanges but by their effect on prices will strike at the whole basis of contract, of security, and of the capitalist system generally."

From the height of their privilege, economic experts discussed inflation as a matter of imbalance between demand and supply in the economy, ultimately boiling down to peoples' *moral* deficiency. Having fought for and obtained higher wages, workers were unable to control themselves and indulged in extravagant behavior, evidenced by "conspicuous increases in unnecessary consumption of alcoholic beverages, sweets, chocolate, and biscuits," as economics professor Luigi Einaudi sneered. With similar disdain, Maffeo Pantaleoni, pioneer of today's mainstream economics, blamed inflation on workers who "live like pigs in their homes in order to waste the greatest part of their income in wine at the tavern."

A few years later, these experts would support the rise to power of the founding father of fascism, Benito Mussolini. Mussolini guaranteed a sufficient dose of economic austerity, characterized by wage reductions, cuts in social spending, the privatization of public services, and increased interest rates. His economic rectitude garnered applause from economic experts worldwide, including liberals and nationalists alike.

Contemporary economists have not renounced the habit of blaming workers. The inclination endures, and a century later the targeted culprits are still those in working-class families.

Let's hop to Washington, DC, in the spring of 2022. Another wave of monetary inflation shakes the global economy. The governing board experts of the Federal Reserve System (the Fed) meet behind closed doors to raise interest rates. They will raise them aggressively for over two years, with tremendous influence over the decisions of central banks worldwide.

Federal Reserve Chairman Jerome Powell and his colleagues have refined their technical language, but the antagonism toward the working classes is no less acute. Powell proclaims that to "restore price stability," economic experts must use their tools "forcefully," and this "will also bring some pain." The *pain* is for the culprits of inflation, namely those who are consuming too much and working too little.

As Powell explains, we are in an "unhealthy" or "tight" labor market, where there are more job openings than there are available people, making it difficult for employers to find employable workers. The goal of raising interest rates is precisely to "have less upward pressure on wages" thanks to the disciplining effect of unemployment. Similarly, US Treasury Secretary Janet Yellen wrote in a memo to then Fed Chairman Alan Greenspan in 1996 that unemployment "serves as a worker-discipline device because the prospect of a costly unemployment spell produces sufficient fear of job loss to motivate workers to perform well without constant, costly supervision."

On September 12, 2023, in his speech at the annual Property Summit of the *Australian Financial Review*, the Australian billionaire and think tank founder Tim Gurner used less subtle words to express comparable thoughts:

> I think the problem that we've had is that people have decided they really didn't want to work so much anymore through COVID, and that has a massive issue on productivity. . . . Unemployment has to jump 40, 50 percent in my view. We need to see pain in the economy. We need to remind people that they work for the employer, not the other way around. . . . We have got to kill that attitude, and that has to come through hurting the economy, which is what the whole global, you know, the world is trying to do. Governments around the world are trying to increase unemployment to get that to some sort of normality, and we're seeing it. . . . We are starting to see less arrogance in the employment market.

Most of us listen to economists and financial leaders with a mix of distraction and resignation. Economic decisions such as interest rate hikes feel like distant scenarios, too technical to directly concern us and over which we can do very little anyway. But is it really so? Or is this ability to "depoliticize" the economy—that is, the ability to deny our participation in economic decision-making—precisely the key to the success of a system that ties our hands and silences our voices? The language economic experts use compels us to think that we don't have the knowledge or authority to partake in fundamental economic decisions that affect our lives. However, when we examine their actions closely, we see that they are engaged in a deeply political project: preserving our economic system—which they regard as the only one possible.

Like the economists of a century ago, modern economists use language that hides an existential concern for a system that is actually neither eternal nor natural. Fear of social disorder shaking the capitalist economy is an unsurprising emotional response if you think your livelihood depends on capitalism.

Obviously, in our society, the vast majority of social relationships are mediated by money. Inflation is frightening precisely because it destabilizes the currency—the foundation on which our entire market economy stands. Not only that, but inflation creates alarm, as Keynes saw, and may erode popular consent for the system. We are outraged to discover that the cost of groceries has doubled or that rising costs of electricity or gasoline might drain our savings. Inflation fuels social discontent, yes, but it can also spark the realization that our economy is not the best possible system in the best possible world.

In 1919, inflation drove citizens in Europe to loot stores, strike, and organize to take control of production. In the post-pandemic economy of the United States, inflation encouraged a push for new unionizations and for unions to demand higher wages. It led employees to question their employers' authority over them through the so-called no-work and quiet quitting movements as well as the "Great Resignation." In 2022 alone, nearly 50 million Americans—a third of all US workers—said "enough" to exploitation by voluntarily leaving their jobs.

Now, as they did a century ago, technocrats look with anxiety at a possible change in the social order and point their fingers at the primary enemy: the workers. But we must not let these false accusations make us feel powerless. Why should we accept an economic system that enriches the extremely wealthy while ordinary people suffer?

The Fight

The decisions of economic institutions, from the Fed to the Treasury in the US to the International Monetary Fund, are not neutral, scientific, or necessarily moral. They have long failed to serve the common good. The idea that the current economic form of our society—what we call capitalism—is something spontaneous, inevitable, and as eternal as gravity is a hoax.

The naturalization of capitalism and our habit of delegating many fundamental decisions to experts render us powerless and strengthen our passive consent to a society that oppresses the majority. Nearly all professional economists, as well as television networks, social media, and newspapers, perpetuate narratives that mask the functioning of our economic system, instead of explaining it. The fact is that the inequities of the system are exploding. In the US, the so-called middle class keeps shrinking while the disparity in wealth grows: the top 0.1 percent owns more than five times the wealth of the bottom 50 percent, and three people have more wealth than 150 million Americans combined. And the problem is not limited to this country. In Britain, the richest 1 percent hold more wealth than 70 percent of the population combined. Since 2014, the number of children living in poverty in the UK has grown to one in three, while in the same period the number of billionaires has sextupled. Globally the superrich saw extraordinary gains in 2022 and 2023: for every $1 of new wealth earned by a person in the bottom 90 percent, each billionaire gained roughly $1.7 million.

Despite claims of job creation, and the dominant message that business success helps all of us, the reality is that ultimately market gains, or profit, are contrary to the well-being of citizens—as one rises, the other decreases. Our current economic system is coercive, and this is the crucial political reality that mainstream economics hides. Even if we feel something is wrong when we get up in the morning to go to a job that means nothing to us, or when we struggle to find time to rest, such an instinctive realization is suffocated by the societal messages that this is the way it should be. The dissonance between our lived experience of daily economic life—that of alienation and struggle—and our acceptance of it, as if there were no alternative, is something *constructed*, predominantly by economic models that reinforce our surrender to an economic system that I call the "capital order." This term refers to, first, the concentration of decision-making power in the hands of private investors; and second, the invisible subjugation of the majority, who are forced to work for someone else's profit.

I wrote this book to expose how that dominant message blinds us to alternative economies. For decades, "experts" have been spreading this numbing story with academic theories spun from the elite circles of the most prestigious universities in the world. By hiding the true nature of the prevailing economic system, they atrophy our minds, blocking any possibility of transformative action. But it is possible to escape from capitalism.

Today's dominant theories are the result of academic and political battles that have lasted hundreds of years, with the aim of expelling the economic paradigm of the founding fathers of political economy. Adam Smith, David Ricardo, and Karl Marx studied capitalism through the lens of class and class conflict. Over the last century, this lens has been replaced by a gaze that substitutes classes with individuals and conflict with harmony. In this rosy world, the engine of growth is not the worker but the entrepreneur who heroically saves and invests. While Smith, Ricardo, and Marx all theorized labor as a key productive class in antagonism with landlords and capitalists, and Marx recognized labor's exploitation as the structural trap of capitalism, neoclassical economists expelled class conflict from their analysis. They posited labor relations as equal exchanges between individuals, imagining a path to prosperity for all those who play their cards right in the game of the free market.

The rise of neoclassical economics at the beginning of the twentieth century portrayed economic theory as being objective. "Pure economics" emerged as the new label for what until then had been known as "political economy." This astute rebranding reimagined an economy that was somehow beyond power relations. Economists became the gatekeepers of infallible models on par with those used by the hard sciences—like, say, Newtonian mechanics—and too sophisticated for most citizens to understand. This coincided with the rise of allegedly politically independent economic institutions such as central banks, which began removing key policy decisions from democratic scrutiny.

The tidying of the economic discourse placed any suggestion of a more human, more commonsensical political project out of bounds. Even well-meaning progressives limit themselves to pointing the finger at exceptional corporate greed or the out-of-control rise of the financial sector. These critiques go nowhere because they ignore the problems within the basic structure. Neoclassical economists have peddled the market society as one in which everyone, if rational and virtuous enough, can thrive. They claim that social hierarchies are reflections of individual merit, meaning that those who aren't at the top don't deserve to be. It is an argument that supports those in power very well.

According to this perspective, the profits of saver-entrepreneurs are the result of their virtuous behavior, enabling them to sign workers' paychecks, which sounds good. The message is so persuasive that today almost everyone has internalized it: if we try hard enough, each of us can become a rich investor. Those who cannot make it can blame only themselves.

Mainstream economic theories have draped obvious absurdities in scientific rigor: those who do not have sufficient resources to make ends meet, because they are unemployed or work for low wages, don't have money to set aside to become a saver-investor. This condition affects the majority of people. More than half of all Americans live in financial insecurity, according to the Urban Institute. Globally, the reality is even bleaker: over half the world's population scrapes by on less than $6.85 a day.

Do we really live in the best and only possible economic reality? During the economic boom of the post–World War II period, a golden age of capitalism, this perspective might have seemed vaguely plausible, at least for those white men living in Europe and the US. However, in the current moment, when the majority of the global population suffers from profound economic and social injustices and the planet is on the brink of ecological collapse, this pseudoscientific best-of-all-possible-worlds idea can't be right. There is a more powerful, humane approach to understanding society.

We must re-democratize the economy so that citizens can reclaim the most important choices that regulate the very foundations of their lives. That is a better way forward than anything capitalism has or can offer. What is the first step in this direction? It is a radical change of perspective. There is nothing more political than the lens through which we view the world. Only if we learn to look at the world differently can we act differently.

This book provides a new emancipatory perspective. The time is ripe to turn toward a truly modern study of economics built from the works of classical political economy. We citizens can use the power of critical economic analysis to break free from the dominant approach to economic policy that places technical expertise above democratic participation and well-being.

My fundamental intuition is that there are no economic problems that are not inevitably also political problems. Contrary to what technocrats typically suggest, our economy is neither a force of nature nor an external object that we can manipulate as if it were a machine. On the contrary, the economy *is us*. Flesh-and-blood people. This means that "capital" as a "commodity," as money to invest, as wealth expressed in gross domestic product, exists thanks to specific social relations, and in particular thanks to the fact that most people have no alternative but to sell their ability to work for a wage and inevitably be paid less than the value they produce. This is the capital order, the backbone to our society that we do not criticize or even discuss. It is only through the lens of class that we can escape this trap and understand the functioning of our economic system and the policies implemented to govern it.

History reveals that, far from being eternal, our economy is fundamentally fragile and based on political decisions that enforce specific social relations. When the central bankers of this world raise interest rates knowing that the practice will cause an economic recession, they do so out of at least one particular concern: if people no longer accept their condition as low-paid wage laborers without secure employment, our economic system would collapse. They are right.

The economy is profoundly political at multiple levels. The

capitalist economic system that oppresses us is political; the economic policies aiming to safeguard and manage it are political; and the economic discipline that provides a lens through which we see the world is political. In the following pages, it will become clear how these three dimensions operate in support of one another.

When we hear the term "political," we mostly associate it with the squabbles between parties and the trivial personalisms of our political class. When I use the term, however, I am asserting something more fundamental: both that the economic world is currently antidemocratic and that it is one in which we can have collective agency. We need not be bound by any supposedly natural and scientific laws dictating that most people must suffer. The economic dimension of our lives is pervasive—it defines who we are as individuals and as a society. But it is also a dimension that we have created. We thus have the power to transform our socioeconomic order into one that does not make us subservient to the interests of the few winners of our current system.

This book is for all those who wake up in the morning with a sense of profound dissatisfaction. I intend to challenge the fatalist notion that nothing can change and the individualist notion that it is all our fault, or the fault of those weaker than us. Instead, I want to clarify that classist economic decisions are the basis of the major problems afflicting our time. I want to clarify the mechanisms that oppress us and identify the freedoms for which we must fight.

All the problems afflicting our era—from the rise of ultranationalist parties to perpetual wars, hatred for migrants, the environmental catastrophe that is especially hitting the Global South, and the mental health crisis, especially among younger people—can be explained by an economic system that oppresses the majority both nationally and globally. When people decide to stop engaging in electoral processes or to vote for parties that present themselves as against the liberal establishment, they are expressing deep dissatisfaction, or even despair, for an economic order that has failed them. These symptoms of our sickly economic order have led to the rise of political figures like President Donald Trump in the US and President Javier Milei in Argentina, who sell themselves as alternatives to the system. But they are false alternatives. The spectacle of strongman personalities distracts us from the fact that their policies are in perfect continuity with capitalism and its austerity logic. At a conservative gathering in 2025, for instance, Milei gifted Trump's then right-hand man Elon Musk with a chainsaw in symbolic support of Musk's proposals to slash nearly all federal funding for the working class, including Medicaid, food stamps, and public schools, especially education programs for low-income communities. These governments' violent leanings are only accelerating capitalism's destructive tendencies toward humanity. Yet people's calls to change the establishment tell me that there is ample space for ambitious, courageous thinking—thinking that envisions radically different principles to govern our society.

In the chapters that follow, we will learn to re-see the way our economic world works, discovering why the same problems seem to arise again and again, and why the usual economic models cannot explain them. Chapter 1 deconstructs the concept of growth, uncovering how this much-celebrated metric produces vast inequality and is grounded on exploitation. Chapter 2 shows the real purpose of austerity and why it is crucial to maintaining the structural oppression that capitalism requires. Chapter 3 subverts the commonsense understanding of unemployment and inflation, revealing how these two enduring social problems are not flaws in our system but are actually core features. Chapter 4 helps us rethink the reasons for the great progress in the US and Europe; it is inseparable from the active creation of poverty in the Global South. And chapter 5 reconsiders the compatibility of democracy and freedom with capitalism. Real democracy requires a completely new worldview.

I write these pages without the detached manner typical of economists. This does not mean abandoning the scientific rigor of investigation. On the contrary, I accept my role as an academic researcher gathering evidence. I accept the unavoidable social positioning of the intellectual, which, as Antonio Gramsci reminds us, is organic to the class struggle. No one who produces knowledge is exempt from the influence of their socioeconomic status: my life, and my place in the world, informs my work. Unlike most economists, therefore, I am aware that I don't exist above the economy, simply observing it; like all other citizens, I live *within* it. I thus try to overcome the limits of my point of view by considering other peoples' historical and contemporary struggles to build a stronger and bigger picture of the economic world we live in. Having done so, I go beyond mere criticism of neoliberalism to propose an anticapitalist view that I hope will shake readers into participating in real social transformation.

As I write, many are fighting for a different society, believing in it with such dedication that they risk their lives. My contribution is from a safe position, but I understand the need for daring. My great-uncle and great-aunt continue to be sources of inspiration. My grandfather Camillo's siblings fought fascist oppression. His sister Teresa Mattei, with the battle name Chicchi, was the youngest woman to sit in the 1946 Italian Constituent Assembly after the fall of Mussolini's regime. It was thanks to her that the words "de facto" were included in Article 3 of the Italian Constitution:

> It is the duty of the Republic to remove the obstacles of an economic and social order, which, by limiting *de facto* the freedom and equality of citizens, prevent the full development of the human person and the effective participation of all workers in the political, economic, and social organization of the country. (my italics)

A free spirit, Teresa began her journey of radicalization when, at the age of sixteen, she stood up from her classroom chair to publicly denounce the antisemitic racial laws that banned Jewish students from Italian public schools. For her defiance, Teresa was permanently expelled from all schools in the Kingdom of Italy, but she retained her bravery to challenge power for the rest of her life. Only six years later, she was uncowed by the violence of the SS Nazi guards when, during the Resistance, they took advantage of her body while she carried messages to her *partigiani* comrades. And when the Communist Party betrayed its ideals, she did not hesitate to walk away, proving that her loyalty was to justice, not to any party line.

Her brother Gianfranco Mattei, a twenty-seven-year-old chemistry professor and member of the anti-Fascist resistance, was captured on February 1, 1944, while building bombs to be used in the fight against the Nazi occupation. After a few days of continuous torture, Gianfranco hanged himself with his belt rather than betray his comrades. The last words of my great-uncle, written on the back of a check secretly handed to his cellmate, were for his parents: "Be strong, knowing that I have been strong too."

To be strong, we need strong tools. To deliver them is my purpose.

1.

THE INVISIBLE ORDER

Let's consider what my concept, the "capital order," means exactly. It is an almost invisible framework. It is so foundational to our lives that we rarely question it. Why do we depend on the market to survive? Why is the satisfaction of our needs mediated by money?

These seem like questions a child might ask. If we're hungry, we're free to go to the supermarket to buy a sandwich. But let's think more about that sandwich. What matters most in our current economic system is not the quality of the mozzarella and ham between the slices of bread, nor the flour the bread is made from, but the price of this food. If we don't have the money, we can't buy it.

This applies to everything in our economy, material or immaterial, from food to housing, transportation to vacations, and even down to the chair I am sitting on right now. They're all commodities, meaning goods endowed with a quantifiable economic value. The "use value" of the commodity—or as economists say, the satisfaction we derive from its use and consumption—is secondary to the "exchange value": that is, the money the producer obtains from its sale. The primary purpose of these commodities is to be sold in exchange for an amount greater than what is invested in their production. Without the expectation of profit, in fact, these commodities would neither be produced nor exchanged. That we organize society through the exchange of commodities is such an obvious reality that it often goes unnoticed. Yet it has a profound impact on our lives: it underlies all the most explosive contradictions in our society.

New York City, where I taught and lived for many years, is one of the wealthiest cities in the world—home to over 349,500 millionaires with a total private wealth that exceeds $3 trillion. Official statistics also note that there are more than 128,000 people living in shelters for the homeless, of which more than 44,000 are children.

It is enough to ride the subway in New York, especially after dinner, to be rattled by scenes of destitution and desperation. The denial of a basic human need, shelter, is a widespread phenomenon in so-called advanced societies. The other half of the paradox is that over sixty thousand apartments are vacant in New York. Super-exclusive skyscrapers, looking like self-important pencils and built on a bedrock of tax breaks, are Gotham's new skyline. The apartments therein are bought and sold by the global elite not to live in but as financial assets. Space is available, and money as well. To solve homelessness through housing construction in California, the state with the largest unhoused population in the country, would require less than 1 percent of the annual US military budget for the next twelve years.

Let's go back to that sandwich. Enough food is produced daily to feed everyone on the planet, yet over 800 million people suffer from hunger. The problem of global hunger has actually worsened in recent years and in 2024 accounted for 45 percent of child deaths worldwide. In developed countries, food insecurity is growing. In the US alone, 13.5 percent of households were food insecure in 2023. However, about one-third of the food produced (1.3 billion tons, with an approximate value of $1 trillion) goes to waste every year because it remains unsold and is thrown away. That much food could feed three billion people. To catch a glimpse of this global reality, it's enough to go to the local supermarket at closing hours: products at or near expiration are discarded. The point is to sell them, not to feed people.

What is irrational according to the logic of needs is entirely rational according to the logic of profits. In the society we live in, the latter prevails over the former. However, nothing is natural or particularly human about the logic of profits. This is not an eternal fact to be passively recorded and accepted; instead, we're talking about a contingent phenomenon that has its own origin and history. Its origin and history need to be interrogated. Understanding them holds emancipatory value.

We live in a *specific* type of economy, with a particular historical form, different from those that preceded it and those that could succeed it. It is thus essential to provide a definition of our economy that is free from technicalities that hide its concrete meaning. Capitalism is a socioeconomic system in which employers use their private means of production to hire wage labor in order to produce commodities whose sale generates profits. The system's two pillars are wage labor and the private means of production. The roof of the system is profit. These two pillars are the attributes of the two main classes that confront each other in society: workers, who live primarily off their labor income, and capitalists, who live primarily off capital income in the form of dividend and interest payments. We're talking about human institutions, generated by precise collective decisions and historical processes that, being human, can be subverted.

The way we explain our society has enormous political repercussions. Economists and economic historians have treated capitalism as the realization of intrinsic and universal human tendencies. To them, our economic system is a mirror of who we really are: self interested individuals who want to maximize our profit. This is false. The concept of profit motive as regulator arose with the advent of modern society. Anthropologists know this well, but anthropologists do not play the central role in our society that economists do.

In the strongly ahistorical mainstream reading, capitalism spontaneously arose and developed through our impulse to maximize self-interest, breaking free from the chains of feudal law and privilege. The upshot of this approach is to internalize the idea that the system we live in today marks "the end of history." Liberal democracy, capitalism's pursuit of profit, and other Western values have established the final, correct form of government and economic structure, as political scientist Francis Fukuyama argued in his influential essay in 1989. If you are persuaded by this argument, the very thought of subverting capitalism becomes unthinkable.

If, instead, we decide to take the historical perspective seriously, if we think that no future scenario is inevitable, two facts become much clearer. First, we are talking about an extremely young system. *Homo sapiens* have been organizing the production of our material conditions for about two hundred thousand years, but industrial capitalism has existed for less than three hundred years. This means that we have lived under capitalism for around 0.1 percent of our history.

Second, capitalism represents a qualitative break from preceding economic systems. The emergence of capitalism created a new social status for the majority of citizens: that of market dependence. Capitalism did not merely come about from a quantitative increase in trade. Markets existed already in antiquity, prior to capitalism. Think about the mosaics that depict the exchange of fruits and more in Roman piazzas. The split comes with the fact that our society now relies on the market for our survival and reproduction. The foundational element of capitalism is a specific class relation. It is exactly this social relationship that allows for economic growth as we know it to occur.

A Prehistory of Capital

The beginning of the historical process that led to today's economic organization was in no way peaceful. It required a violent expropriation of people's means of subsistence on a large scale, which laid the groundwork for the emergence of the social relation at the core of our society: the wage relation.

The processes of forced expropriation varied significantly in their historical contexts. In countries of the Americas and Africa, for instance, the original accumulation of capital is intimately linked to centuries-long colonization. Starting from the fifteenth century, European powers appropriated land, resources, and human beings, disrupting indigenous economic systems in the process.

For example, the North American people known as the Cherokee had a communal, stewardship-based relationship with the land—one fundamentally at odds with the individualistic, extractive relationship dominating today. They cultivated land collectively, and in their matrilineal social system cultivation was foremost the purview of women. Contact with white settlers provoked a shift in their relation to land. Tribal leaders began to divide and sell it in exchange for arms and beads and were forced to accept treaties that ceded land to the settlers. A fundamental turning point came with the Indian Removal Act of 1830, which laid the groundwork for a process of mass dispossession that culminated in the Trail of Tears—a thousand-mile march to "Indian Territory" (now Oklahoma) during which approximately four thousand Cherokee died from disease, starvation, and exposure.

The archetypal process of forced expropriation originated in Britain, the cradle of capitalism. In fifteenth-century Britain, the majority of the population consisted of free peasant farmers, who were subjects of feudal lords but had access to their means of subsistence. The farmers had the right to cultivate a plot of land and had free entry to the common land: meadows for grazing, forests for gathering wood, and so on.

They were living within the socioeconomic system that flourished and consolidated in Europe between the ninth and fifteenth centuries: feudalism. Holding a feudal title did not equate to owning land as private property. Land was not yet a commodity that lords could freely buy and sell. Rather, they inherited control of the estates or were granted the title to their land as a reward for political loyalty or military service, and such a transfer conferred usage rights but not ownership as we think of it.

Starting from the late fifteenth century, a tumultuous process of privatization changed things radically. It involved violent acts of dispossession by a new generation of feudal lords who privatized the common lands to which subjects previously had access. Shared resources were transformed into the private property of a small minority. By 1600, a significant portion of cultivable land in England was already enclosed, with less than 30 percent still held in common. This process was soon endorsed by the English Parliament. Parliament passed the Enclosure Acts, establishing enforcement mechanisms for this mass privatization.

Far from being spontaneous, our economic system was built by state institutions. In Britain, without laws—the political decisions of the elite sitting in Parliament—there would have been no recognition of land, which was the most important means of production at that time, as private property. The presumed naturalness and even "sanctity" of the second pillar of capitalism, private ownership of the means of production, has been politically constructed and shaped over time.

But our economic system would be stillborn without the emergence of the first pillar of capitalism, wage labor—the novel social condition of the majority of the population. This class of dispossessed wage laborers was formed by the centuries-long process of enclosure of the common land. It's no surprise that a transition from one socioeconomic system to another takes generations, is richly layered, and is marked by tumultuous social upheavals. But I want to emphasize one aspect of this transition that immediately imposed itself: the inseparable connection between the increase in wealth of a few on one hand, and the dizzying growth of poverty among the majority on the other. The wealth of nations (also the title of the famous book by Adam Smith published in 1776) generated through capital accumulation was only made possible through exploitation and impoverishment of the masses. The philosopher Richard Price, in 1771, explained that when the common land got into the hands of a few great farmers, the majority of little farmers

> will be converted into a body of men who earn their subsistence by working for others, and who will be under a necessity of going to market for all they want. . . . There will, perhaps, be more labour, because there will be more compulsion to it. . . . Towns and manufactures will increase, because more will be driven to them in quest of places and employment. This is the way in which the engrossing of farms actually operates. And this is the way in which, for many years, it has been actually operating in this kingdom.

Intellectuals and scholars who observed the nascent capitalist system highlighted the emergence of "pauperism," a phenomenon inexorably linked to land privatization. The state intervened with aggressive legislation to discipline those deprived of their means of subsistence. Poverty became stigmatized, shameful, a personal fault. Henry VIII, king of England and lord of Ireland from 1509 to 1547, granted a begging license to elderly and disabled beggars but had no mercy for able-bodied vagabonds, who were sentenced to whipping and imprisonment. The Vagabonds Act of 1547 went even further, stipulating that anyone who denounced an individual as refusing to work could claim them as a slave. During the reign of Queen Elizabeth I in 1572, Parliament amended the law, establishing that beggars over the age of fourteen without a license should be severely whipped and branded with a hot iron on the lobe of the left ear. In case of repeat offenders, if over the age of eighteen, they were to be executed.

By the mid-nineteenth century, the machinery of capitalism was perfected. Private property and wage relations were no longer seen as historical institutions that evolved at the expense of other systems; they represented the natural order of things.

Let's stress a crucial, ironic point: while in many socioeconomic systems preceding capitalism the political relationship of subjugation of the majority was explicit and evident, with capitalism, the idea that all citizens enjoy political and economic freedom emerged. Through the various processes that deprived people of their means of subsistence, most individuals have become "free workers." But what does "free" mean in this usage? It encapsulates what is truly distinct about our economic system from those that preceded it. Our status as free wage workers is indeed different; we are free to contract our labor with whomever we wish. Unlike slaves in the time of the Romans, today we are emancipated citizens. We are not anyone's property; we are not bound by social hierarchies established by birth; we are equal and free citizens before the law. However, we are also "free" in a second sense: we have been "freed" from our means of subsistence. Having lost the right to access land, other common goods, and more generally our means of production, we now depend on wage labor. This means that we are not free economically.

While a small minority primarily lives off capital income—for example, on dividends from stock ownership, interest payments from debt holdings, capital gains on the sale of appreciated assets, or rental income—most of us don't. We have no option but to sell our own ability to work to earn our way through life. In other words, we make a living by possessing a fundamental commodity—our ability to work—and we sell it on the market in exchange for the wage on which our survival depends.

Class

The majority of the population sells their labor as a commodity for money in order to buy other commodities such as food, rent, utilities, cell phone service, insurance, and transport. This is the hidden framework of our dependence on the market, and it is a form of implicit coercion. It is less visible, less contestable, and therefore easier to pass off as an indisputable fact of life.

In the feudal system, a serf had independent access to their means of production and would surrender part of the product of their labor to the lord because of the status of the latter and out of fear of personal retaliation. Today a Starbucks employee signs a work contract without facing personal pressure; rather, the pressure arises from their economic need. The peculiarity of capitalism stems from the fact that, unlike in previous class-based societies, the coercion it exerts is impersonal: there is no hierarchical figure compelling us to sell our labor. It is much simpler: if we don't enter the labor market, we don't survive.

In our society, the state's redistributive interventions (such as health care, subsidized housing, or unemployment benefits) have very clear political limits: they cannot go so far as to violate the premise of market dependence. If governments were to do so, they would jeopardize a main pillar of our economy: wage labor. The constraint on any potential universal basic income reform is that it must not in any way disincentivize citizens from working for a wage. In other words, political action cannot challenge the economic system. Even the famous American New Deal was carefully structured to avoid unconditional cash transfers (maligned as "the dole"), and public works programs were explicitly designed as emergency measures rather than features of a permanent welfare state. Popular demands, meanwhile, may focus on introducing a wealth tax or strengthening workers' rights, but abolishing private property and wage labor seems like an idea from science fiction.

Today, increasingly impoverished governments frequently sell land from which many of their citizens derive sustenance, plunging them into new forms of market dependence. In the twenty-first century, the race for land in countries in the south of the globe, especially in Africa, has intensified. According to the World Bank, from 2008 to 2012, more than 138 million acres worldwide—nearly double the size of Italy—were subject to "land deals." Large multinational corporations buy land from the government or directly from poor farmers and impose evictions. Indigenous activists fight this land grabbing daily and often lose their lives.

In 2020, India witnessed the largest strike in world history, involving 250 million workers, mostly in the agricultural sector, which employs over half of the country's workforce. Among other things, farmers demanded a halt to the privatization of agricultural land. Land acquisition in India has accelerated in the past thirty-five years: the number of displaced people more than doubled between 1990 and 2004, from slightly under 30 million to 60 million. Of the total land acquired between 1947 and 2004, more than half was forested areas and common property, disproportionately affecting small subsistence farmers. If the global labor force has increased by more than a billion people since 1980, that has in part been through the destruction of alternative means of making a living.

Corporations and states will always seek out new frontiers of privatization—such as water, or genetically engineered seeds—that lock in our dependence on the market. The expropriation of the means of subsistence is a phenomenon that never stops: it constitutes the lifeblood of capitalism. Marx saw the brutality of this:

The historical movement which changes the producers into wage-labourers appears, on the one hand, as their emancipation from serfdom and from the fetters of the guilds, and it is this aspect of the movement which alone exists for our bourgeois historians. But, on the other hand, these newly freed men became sellers of themselves only after they had been robbed of all their own means of production, and all the guarantees of existence afforded by the old feudal arrangements. And this history, the history of their expropriation, is written in the annals of mankind in letters of blood and fire.

To step back far enough to see this hidden coercive system that capitalism has engineered, we need the concept of class. My approach draws inspiration from the works of the great masters of political economy, Adam Smith, David Ricardo, and Karl Marx—authors I have had the pleasure of teaching my students at the New School for Social Research in New York and the University of Tulsa. The works of these classical economists have provided us with a lens capable of explaining the society in which we live, its mechanisms, and its deep structure. It's important that we explore their concepts for our current developments.

"Class" is often used to describe differences in wealth, self-perception, and social status. This can be misleading. Income levels, education, lifestyles, and consumption patterns are parameters used to divide the population in a society where belonging to the so-called middle class is considered to be the healthy norm, with some excesses represented on one side by the small number of millionaires at the top of the social pyramid and on the other side by the group of poor people living at the bottom. According to the dominant narrative, the majority of us belong to the middle class, whose crisis is recounted with bitterness and disappointment, while the very idea of the existence of a working class is dismissed as a rusty, useless notion of a dead and buried ideology.

Class conflict is the dramatic plot that society is missing—like an audience in a cinema mesmerized by the actors' performances and the filmmaker's art but failing to see the movie's deeper story. Economic measurements such as the size of your bank account are merely the faces, the costumes, of more fundamental dynamic forces: namely our relationship with our work, the fruits of that labor, and the means of production. Here are the essential questions to ask yourself regarding class:

1. Where does the majority of your income come from: invested capital or wages?
2. Do you control the production processes, or have you had to relinquish control as a result of your employment contract?

Those who control the means of production, who dictate the conditions of others' work, or who own capital that can be invested in production are part of the capitalist class. Those who must sell their labor power—their capacity to work—for a wage because they lack access to the means of production, are hired to perform tasks they do not control, or have no claim to the product they generate, belong to the working class.

Economists Lance Taylor and Özlem Ömer show that in

the United States, the capitalist class represents the wealthiest 1 percent of the population. These are individuals who primarily live off capital income generated by the wealth they own, such as dividends and interest. A much larger portion of the population relies mainly on income generated from their labor, and there is also a smaller segment of the population that lives on low wages and social benefits. In 2024, 77 percent of American workers reported that they would have financial difficulty if their paycheck was delayed by just one week. In a society where we increasingly depend on the market for everything, one out of three Americans is forced to postpone or forgo medical care because they cannot afford it, often with mortal consequences. This forgoing of medical care happens even in European countries with better health systems. In 2023, 7.6 percent of the Italian population gave up medical treatment because it was too expensive or the wait list for it was excessively long. We're talking about approximately four million Italians.

This data paints a very different picture from the one that portrays industrialized Western societies as centered on the middle class. Poverty cannot be passed off as a temporary condition of people living in the Global South (representing an astonishing seven billion out of the eight billion inhabitants of the planet) whose lot will soon improve thanks to economic growth and development. On the contrary, poverty is inherent to the very nature of capitalist society even in its most developed form. Even in the richest country in the world, the United States, during its golden post–World War II epoch, poverty was pervasive. In 1962, it plagued 20 percent of American families (around 35 million individuals) and almost half of the nonwhite population.

The emphasis on class does not minimize other forces shaping social hierarchies, such as racial oppression. Clearly, important social differences exist beyond the fact that Black American workers earn 25 percent less than their white counterparts. Black Americans are incarcerated, sentenced to death, and victimized by predatory loans at much higher rates than white Americans with the same economic status. However, focusing on class dynamics helps illuminate those power structures that are constitutive of capitalism and for this very reason typically swept under the rug. Class and racial oppression are inextricable. The history of slavery and systemic racism codified under Jim Crow has long dispossessed Black Americans of their means of production, resulting in white Americans having over six times more wealth than Black Americans. It is no coincidence that only 1 percent of the top 1 percent of Americans are Black. The majority of Black American households are also Black American working-class households.

The economic lens that focuses on the concept of class certainly does not ignore that classes are fluid and take shape in a variety of ways. Within the same class, social differences exist. The small owner of a local pharmacy does not occupy the same position as the CEO of a multinational pharmaceutical company; similarly, being a middle manager in a large corporation is quite different from being a precarious worker with constantly expiring contracts.

In other words, the class lens does not represent a false two-dimensional reality; instead, it allows for an accurate account of the variety of social positions and also the historical changes that have transformed our economic system. The economist Friedrich Engels was born in 1820 to a textile magnate father. At that time, his father, as a capitalist, owned his own factories and directly managed production. Since then, the capitalist system's tendency toward division of labor has generated more complex situations in which ownership and management of the company are typically separated. As a rule, the major shareholders are not the CEOs of a company. The former can delegate their administrators—especially asset managers today, who will plan investments—while the latter will work hard, receiving high salaries and benefiting from lavish stock options (that corporations promote to achieve large tax breaks) and other perks. Apple's CEO Tim Cook, for example, whose compensation package hit almost $75 million in 2024—including a $3 million base salary and $58 million in stock awards—is known for his tireless work ethic. No doubt, top managers work. However, their role is qualitatively different from the role of wage workers. The class lens shows us how the two types of workers respond to different logics.

We saw how the working class operates according to the behavioral logic: ability to work leads to money in your paycheck that leads to consuming goods. But what about the class of those people who manage investments and control the production process?

Growth

The logical progression of the capitalist class is based on growth. Growth is a kind of Trojan horse. What a lovely gift growth appears to be! Newspaper headlines hold it dear. "Annual US Budget: Won't Affect Growth"; "Reckoning with an Era of Slow Growth"; "Less Taxes for Growth." Gross domestic product (GDP), the total value of the final goods and services produced in a country, is the most cited measurement quantifying growth. With GDP, economists and politicians have found a metric that perfectly suits the characteristics of our economy. GDP exalts capitalism's qualities, such as its historic ability to produce great expansion of wealth. And of course it hides its limitations, most egregiously how unevenly this wealth is actually distributed and the environmental toll of producing such wealth. Indeed, even as GDP grows, wealth concentration has hit historic highs: in 2024 alone, the world's billionaires added $2 trillion to their wealth—equivalent to $5.7 billion per day—while almost half the world is in poverty, living on less than $6.85 per day.

Neoclassical economists teach us that the economy works well if it grows because capitalism thereby blesses us with accelerating progress. Previously unimaginable innovations, from dishwashers to home computers to polio vaccines, do improve our daily lives. But there are hidden and unnecessary costs. In a system based on increasing monetary value, positive results for people are mere byproducts of economic operations whose main objective is profit.

But this is not the whole story. The version of society that experts impose on us puts us in a chokehold. To satisfy our needs, we depend on a system whose logic is not only indifferent to them but also requires our exploitation. Economic growth is produced by a specific social order in which the majority of citizens are compelled to sell their labor power in exchange for a wage that is less than the value they produce. This means that the profits generated by workers form the basis of economic growth. This is a fundamental characteristic of the society we live in, what I call the capital order.

Economic growth is the outcome of capital accumulation following a narrow behavioral logic. The capitalist class invests money to produce consumable goods in order to obtain more money. Thus our economy is oriented toward the constant growth of profits. Note that this abstract logic inverts the daily behavior of market-dependent workers who trade their commodity (labor power) for money so as to buy consumable goods. The feudal lord consumed the wealth produced by serfs by hosting sumptuous banquets or financing the construction of conspicuous symbols that demonstrated his power to the outside world, such as churches and palaces. The paramount objective of, say, Henry Ford was not to consume the cars he produced, or luxury goods he could afford thanks to the success of his business, but to increase his profit. The purpose of capital investment and capital accumulation is not to use the product but to make more money than one started with. When money is the end goal, its accumulation is potentially infinite.

Capitalist profit is not just commercial profit, which comes from buying cheaply and selling at a higher price. This process was already present in precapitalist societies. Even in a mercantilist system, the infamous British East India Company bought tea and silk from its colonies to sell at a markup in the homeland. Commercial profit still forms the pivot on which financial speculation is based. However, the secret power of capitalist accumulation is mainly based on a different process. All goods are exchanged at their fair value. No one is cheating anyone. So in a properly capitalist system, where do these profits come from? The answer shows why capitalist wealth is grounded in inequality and human alienation.

Class exploitation is not tied to low wages, has nothing to do with the indiscriminate mistreatment of some workers, and cannot simplistically be attributed to the immorality of employers. Morality is irrelevant; the crucial point lies elsewhere. All wage labor, even if it pays well, is by definition exploited labor because, counterintuitively, we as workers produce more value than we receive in our paychecks. "Exploitation" is a term that captures the essence of the wage relationship between worker and employer. The slogan "A fair day's wage for a fair day's work" is a hoax. It is not enough to increase wages and obtain better working conditions to free oneself from exploitation.

Exploitation occurs when producers are deprived of what they produce. In other words, employees do not have control over the product of their labor and must surrender it to their employers. Again, the feudal lord lived by seizing a portion of the grain grown by the serf. In slave societies, slave owners appropriated the cotton harvested by the enslaved. As we have seen, this appropriation occurred openly, through political means. Capitalist exploitation, however, is implicit, and we have come to overlook its extraordinary power over us.

From the perspective of the labor market, the wage earner has a legally analogous position to that of the employer and is formally free to choose among various possibilities, including leisure. No one will force her to work. If we are in a favorable moment, as wage earners, we can choose the best offer and sign the contract. Neoclassical economists see workers as rational agents perfectly capable of deciding to maximize their utility. In their models, wages correspond to the marginal productivity of the work performed, which means that workers deserve exactly what they receive in their paycheck. There is no exploitation, no expropriation. Everything is good and fair.

This interpretation represents the dominant story today. It is one constructed with stubborn precision by economists and politicians throughout at least the last century, and it empties and mystifies the very concept of profit. Like wage workers, capitalists should indeed be remunerated for the value they produce through capital investment. Wages and profit are really the same thing. End of story.

From the perspective of the market, the capitalist behaves like any other buyer. With his initial capital, he buys the commodities necessary for production, including a special commodity we will call labor power. Labor power is people's ability to work. It is what you sell to your employer when you sign your contract with them: in return for a wage, you agree that within certain hours of the day you will use this ability in service to their business. The capitalist pays for the commodity of labor power at a price that varies. If the bargaining power of wage earners is high—perhaps due to low unemployment—then the price of labor power will also be high. This increases workers' illusion that they are being fairly compensated for their work.

But the illusion breaks down once we leave the sphere of the labor market and enter that of production. Capitalists have the right to fully "consume" this special commodity they have purchased. Consuming labor power means putting you to work, work that generates value. And it turns out that this work produces much more value than what you get in your paycheck. This extra value, or more technically surplus value, is the source of profit and economic growth in a capitalist economy.

The fundamental point is that surplus value is generated by unpaid labor, and this is a characteristic of the system: without it, there would be no profit for the employer. Without profit, there would be no capital accumulation, no economic growth, and fundamentally no capitalism. The capitalist pays for the commodity of labor power, but not for the value workers actually produce. For example, during their eight-hour shift, Kellogg's factory workers produce cereals and snacks worth thousands of dollars but are paid only $120 a day. A Starbucks employee may be paid $100 a day, but in the same period they may sell $1,000 worth of coffee, generating profits that go directly to the multinational corporation. In both cases, employees keep working long after the value they have generated for the company covers their wages. In other words, capital expands not through equal exchange, as the market perspective suggests, but precisely through its opposite: by not paying workers for a portion of their labor.

An Instagram video brilliantly portrays what's at stake in an imagined exchange between an employer and critical observer:

EMPLOYER: I pay her to be here. Her time is mine right now.
OBSERVER: How much do you pay her?

EMPLOYER: Seven twenty-five an hour.
OBSERVER: Huh. How much product does she make in an hour?
EMPLOYER: On average, ten.
OBSERVER: How much do you make off of those ten?
EMPLOYER: After input costs, probably twenty dollars.
OBSERVER: Sounds like she's paying you twelve seventy-five an hour.

There is another aspect that our class lens clarifies. Profit is driven not only by unpaid wage labor but also by the unpaid labor that takes place outside the company and ensures the physical and psychological well-being of the worker. We are talking about domestic work in the home, like cooking and cleaning and mending, as well as health care and schooling through which workers can build skills used in their jobs. These are essential costs for the healthy maintenance of the workforce, but the capitalist does not have to bear them (and may actually profit from delivering these essential services). As feminist historian Tithi Bhattacharya writes, echoing an important debate in the field of feminist political economy:

> The working class doesn't only work in its workplace. A woman worker also sleeps in her home, her children play in the public park and go to the local school, and sometimes she asks her retired mother to help out with the cooking. In other words, the major functions of reproducing the working class take place outside the workplace.

The capitalist system is driven to increase exploitation as much as possible, or rather the rate of exploitation, which is the ratio between surplus value and the cost of labor power. Can this be attributed to capitalists' greed? Again, the answer is no. The irrelevance of greed reveals the force of market dependence. The system has commandeered our behavior. Morality, good or bad, has lost its agency.

Competition

To realize a profit, it is not enough to exploit workers and thus obtain commodities that embody greater value than the originally invested capital; these commodities must also be sold. However, a sale is by no means guaranteed. Businesses find themselves in competition. For their business to survive, they must sell their goods more effectively than others who have exactly the same objective. While central planning may prevail within a corporation (managers decide the general level of production and hiring), this is not the case at the level of our economy. There is no planning regarding what is produced and distributed or what is socially necessary. The New York City Council does not meet to discuss how many apples and how many shoes New Yorkers need for the month and figure out how to deliver them to their homes. The market is anarchic. Any one business produces whatever it likes so long as it can stay afloat. Competition is a continuous battle. Every business must struggle within an environment it does not control; and even if it could control, say, the weather, it still couldn't control its competitors.

Our recent history is full of companies that have failed because they couldn't prevail over their competitors. Blockbuster was a multibillion-dollar entertainment company dedicated to selling and renting videotapes, with over nine thousand stores worldwide and sixty thousand employees. The company completed its trajectory rather abruptly when it failed to keep pace with streaming technologies. Executives missed the opportunity to purchase what was then a small company named Netflix, unaware that soon most people would watch their favorite shows and movies over the internet. Thus, Netflix replaced Blockbuster.

The pressure of that kind of real competition drives up the rate of exploitation. Researchers have calculated that the rate of exploitation of workers to produce the iPhone X (the 2017 model) is twenty-five times higher than that in nineteenth-century factories at the dawn of the Industrial Revolution. The same researchers have also highlighted another fact: if Apple were to produce the iPhone in the United States instead of the Global South, where it can leverage low wages and inhumane working conditions, it would have to sell each phone for $30,000 instead of $900 to maintain the same level of profit.

One way to increase the rate of exploitation is to extend the working day (what Marxian economists call absolute surplus value), but this can go only so far. Of course, the working day cannot be extended to the point of annihilating the physical reproduction of workers. Workers have to sleep, eat, and stay healthy enough to show up to work, or at least enough of them do to avoid a labor shortage.

Another barrier to increasing the length of the working day

is that workers have been able to assert themselves. During the nineteenth century and much of the twentieth, workers fought to pressure governments to regulate the working day. In Britain, for example, the limit of eight hours per day was a victory of the post–World War I period, a time when strikes reached unprecedented levels. Unfortunately, in recent decades we have witnessed a real regression. With the transition to the so-called gig economy, for many, working hours have become so flexible as to seem endless.

There are less explicit, and therefore less politically contestable, methods to increase the rate of exploitation. They all involve keeping the length of the workday constant but reducing the "paid" portion of it (what Marxian economists call relative surplus value). In this way, the worker increases the amount of unpaid labor that enriches the employer. Hence, the surplus value generated by workers increases. As we shall see, this can be done by increasing productivity, repressing wages, or increasing labor intensity.

During the so-called golden age of capitalism, the decades following World War II until the oil crisis in 1973, the dynamism of the economic system was primarily ensured by technological innovation, aimed at increasing labor productivity and thus fueling the growth of relative surplus value. Increasing labor productivity means that, within the same time frame, each worker produces more value. The Ford factory model, in which work modes and times are standardized, and where every activity and even physical movement is scientifically planned, fueled the increase in profits, not by resorting to wage repression but by intervening through technological innovation. This was the key to the economic miracle in Western countries in the 1950s and 1960s, when productivity grew faster than real wages, and thus the improvement in workers' living conditions was compatible with an increase in profits. To clarify, when economists speak of real wages, they refer to the purchasing power of money, taking into account inflation, which is distinct from nominal wages, or the amount of money in one's paycheck.

Relative surplus value can also be generated by simply cutting wages, even below subsistence levels. This seemingly self-defeating practice is increasingly common. According to a recent report analyzing salary data against MIT's Living Wage Calculator, more than 44 percent of American full-time workers do not make enough to meet basic needs. The number of people who fall into the category of the "working poor" is on the rise globally. In the United States, McDonald's and Walmart (the two largest private employers in the world) pay so little that their workers have to rely on state aid for the poor to survive, from Medicaid to food stamps. The numbers are discouraging. An official report for Congress states that in 2020, 70 percent of Americans receiving state aid were full-time employees. New data also shows that more than half of the homeless population is employed. I spoke to a cashier at the chain store the Dollar Tree in Tulsa who is homeless. She makes nine dollars an hour, and she can work only twenty hours per week because the Dollar Tree limits employee hours to avoid paying benefits. Especially in societies where the economy is increasingly based on the service sector, where there is little room for investment in technological development to increase labor productivity, suppressing wages remains the dominant strategy to increase the rate of exploitation.

A third strategy is the use of monitoring technologies to force employees to simply work harder: that is, to keep work intensity high. Today, Amazon is the vanguard in this inhuman technology. "I was a picker and we were expected to always pick 400 units [packages] within the hour," said Juan Espinoza, an Amazon employee interviewed by *The Guardian*. "I couldn't handle it. I'm a human being, not a robot." Ilya Geller, another employee added: "You're being tracked by a computer the entire time you're there. You don't get reported or written up by managers. You get written up by an algorithm. . . . You're keenly aware there is an algorithm keeping track of you, making sure you keep going as fast as you can, because if there is too much time lapsed between items, the computer will know this, will write you up, and you will get fired." The production model of Amazon is based on a constant turnover of personnel who leave due to excessive psycho-physical stress.

Economist and former Greek minister of finance Yanis Varoufakis offers a powerful image of the accelerating onslaught of these technological advancements:

> Workers forced to work for these algorithms find themselves in a modernist nightmare: some non-corporeal entity that not only lacks but is actually incapable of human empathy allocates them work at a rate of its choosing before monitoring their response times. . . . The workers sacked by the algorithm are thrown into a Kafkaesque spiral, unable to speak to a human capable of explaining why they were fired.

The extent to which economic success hinges on increasing the rate of exploitation, and how much it matters to maintain the dominance of a giant like Amazon, is evident from the amount of capital that its executive chairman, Jeff Bezos, has chosen to invest in recent years to prevent unionization by employees who've primarily demanded a more humane workload. In the spring of 2022, Amazon's anti-union campaign in Bessemer, Alabama, made headlines worldwide for the ferocity with which it silenced Black women who reported not having enough time during breaks to go to the bathroom.

The injuries from overwork and consequent deaths are a constant in the history of our economic system and continue even in the most advanced economies. In Italy, a country with a higher unionization rate than the US, there were three workplace deaths per day in 2024. So long as other workers are available to take their place, concerns for the health and safety of workers have no part in the logic of capital accumulation.

Technological evolution is obviously good in many ways. It is the common measure of success of our system and has brought capitalist society unprecedented material growth. This fact is undeniable, and it is also the favorite weapon of politicians and economists to assert categorically that there can be no better model than the current one.

Marx was himself a great admirer of the triumph of the modern bourgeoisie, the protagonist of a change that demolished ancient power relations and privileges and produced remarkable scientific discoveries. "The bourgeoisie," he wrote, "cannot exist without constantly revolutionising the instruments of production, and thereby the relations of production, and with them the whole relations of society."

Technological innovation is integral to our system because it is a necessary means to advance in competition. It might seem like capitalists have the freedom to decide whether they should invest in technology to boost productivity. But this is not so. Rather, companies feel market pressure to increase productivity just to keep up with their competitors. Thus it is not just workers who are bound by impersonal forces but also the owners of the means of production. Those who do not innovate fail to secure profits, and therefore do not survive as capitalists.

The first companies that manage to increase labor productivity, and therefore relative surplus value, can lower prices to gain competitive advantage without reducing profits. They will capture new market shares, sidelining competitors. Alternatively, by maintaining the same prices, entrepreneurs will make supernormal profits that ensure further economic advantage. In fact, the additional capital obtained can be reinvested in other technological innovations for new conquests. However, it is not certain that the advantageous situation will last forever. Competitors will soon catch up by adopting similar innovations, and before long, all producers will be able to create a similar commodity in less time. The race for innovation and the tendency to lower prices cannot be stopped. To maintain their competitive edge, winning companies must reinvest profits in new production cycles. The winners concentrate capital and expand, engulfing smaller fish.

Walmart was born as a discount store in Arkansas, United

States, in 1962. In its first decade, it recorded 3.5 new store openings per year. In the following decade, the number of stores opened increased tenfold, jumping to 42.7 per year. In the third decade, it reached 129.4 new openings per year in the United States alone. In its sixty-one years of existence, Walmart has grown from a single store to a chain of 10,623 locations worldwide, selling any merchandise and obtaining the title of the world's leading retailer, a primacy currently being contested by Amazon. It is no coincidence that Walmart workers earn about 14.5 percent less than others in the same retail sector. And it is no coincidence that, as noted, it employs the highest number of workers who are beneficiaries of public food subsidies. Research has also found that "when Wal-Mart entered a county, the total wage bill declined along with the average wage. Factoring in both the impact on wages and jobs, the total amount of retail earnings in a county fell by 1.5 percent for every new Wal-Mart store."

Over the years, Walmart has put local mom-and-pop shops out of business. Similarly, the automotive industry in the United States has seen hundreds of entities succumb over the years, either absorbed or pushed out of the market, leading to a sector now dominated by three major multinational corporations: Ford, General Motors, and Stellantis, recently in the spotlight for a clash with employees demanding higher wages and shorter workweeks.

In just a couple of decades, Google has transformed from a simple search engine into an online behemoth. Between 2001 and 2022, it completed over 250 acquisitions, mostly of small software companies. Now it averages one acquisition per week, controls about three-quarters of the digital-search advertising market, and is expanding into new territories such as health care technologies, and artificial intelligence. Amazon, originally a book retailer, has acquired over one hundred different businesses in the last ten years.

It is important to point out that capitalists compete at 360 degrees: for market shares within their sectors and against other capitalist factions. Workers' exploitation generates a pool of value in the economy, which various capitalists appropriate. This leads to conflicts among industrialists, merchants, financiers, and landowners, with each faction eager to dispossess others of their asset values by any means necessary. The dominance of one faction over the others shifts throughout different historical phases, significantly impacting labor relations.

In recent decades, merchant corporations like Ikea, Costco, Gap, and Zara and electronics companies like Apple have appropriated large chunks of value from industrialists by pressuring them to reduce prices, significantly contributing to poor labor conditions across the globe. It's no surprise that the garment industry's fast-fashion clothes are made in sweatshops.

As the famous Marxian scholar David Harvey points out, an observer flying through time would be unable to see the difference between the working conditions in cotton mills of 1840s Manchester that Marx and Engels reported and in the Rana Plaza textile and apparel factory complex, twenty miles outside Dhaka in Bangladesh, which collapsed in 2013, killing 1,129 workers, mostly women, and wounding many more. Producing textiles and name-brand apparel for Western markets, the factories inside Rana Plaza were under constant pressure to cut costs for the benefit of Western consumers. The same could be said of the Foxconn production complexes in China, which produce most of Apple's products and employ over seven hundred thousand people. A spate of worker suicides in 2011 at the Shenzhen factory—called "Foxconn City"—compelled Foxconn to install netting on the cramped company-provided living quarters of the migrant workers to capture anyone who jumped.

The dynamic of merchant capitalists disciplining industrial ones takes on wholly new dimensions within the privatized cloud spaces where Amazon Web Services and Microsoft Azure construct algorithms that work for their bottom lines. The industrial capitalists who produce goods to sell on these platforms are now policed by the cloud services. A click (or an automated decision by an algorithm) is enough to exclude industrial capitalists from their markets, forcing them to hand over costly rents or risk operational shutdown. Thus the pressure to stay in business by increasing the rate of exploitation intensifies.

The centralization of winners extends to all sectors, including health insurance, pharmaceuticals, and finance, where a few banks like JPMorganChase dominate and buy out others. The new frontier of centralization is that of asset management firms, major speculators who invest capital on behalf of others, lately with a particular interest in "green sectors" and infrastructure. In the wake of the 2008 crisis, as the US government absorbed financial risks and restructured the financial sector, three asset management firms, BlackRock, Vanguard, and State Street, displaced the banks as the most powerful financial institutions. The firms accumulated "ownership with a power and scale never seen before in the history of capitalism," according to political economists Stephen Maher and Scott Aquanno. Together, the Big Three in asset management are the largest single shareholders in almost 90 percent of the firms listed on the New York Stock Exchange, including Apple, Microsoft, ExxonMobil, General Electric, and Coca-Cola. Their portfolio encompasses 98 percent of firms on the S&P 500 Index, which tracks the largest American companies—with the Big Three owning an average of more than 20 percent of each company.

The processes of centralization and concentration feed into each other. The larger you are, the more investors you will attract, and the more credit you will receive at advantageous interest rates from banks. At the same time, state support will increase by way of tax breaks and various economic benefits. Hence the emergence of what is commonly referred to as the monopolistic power of large conglomerates.

But as winners pile up victories, they can't stop competing. Attempts to alleviate the burden of real competition through political concessions never fully work. Amazon fiercely opposes its workers' demands for more humane conditions because its advantageous position is not secure. Its competitors, such as eBay and Alibaba, could at any moment surpass it by increasing relative surplus value through lower wages, more efficient robots, and algorithms. All of a sudden, Amazon would stop being so attractive to big shareholders, who might divert their capital elsewhere. Executives of companies that are listed on the stock markets are pressured and incentivized to constantly increase profits, and thus increase dividends and share prices. The growing capital mobility of asset managers only strengthens these disciplinary dynamics of market dependence. Real competition keeps capitalism in a constant state of flux as businesses rush to gain efficiency, increase the rate of exploitation, and bankrupt those who can't keep pace.

But isn't competition supposed to be a good thing? Respected analysts and pundits tell us that the current problem is the lack of competition. According to their perspective, the market is not a place where there's stifling compulsion to increase profits and market share and the tendency toward capital concentration; rather, it's the key to preventing—through the noble tool of competition—lobbies and corporations from indiscriminately enjoying rents. In academic parlance, "rents" refers to the extra amount you pay for any resource beyond what it cost to make it. Free competition, if truly safeguarded, would eliminate rents and bring out the best of both firms and workers. However, this rhetoric is largely the outcome of idealized, pseudoscientific economic models, not always done in good faith. These models and their idealized notions of competition prevent us from seeing the real condition of the society we live in.

While the processes we have discussed so far highlight the real warlike nature of competition among capitalists, neoclassical economics has preferred to embrace a gross abstraction, a perfect world of equilibrium in which firms act harmoniously, guided by the invisible hand of the market. As Anwar Shaikh, a prominent economist who has had a profound impact in revitalizing the tradition of classical political economy, puts it, "The capitalism they [neoclassical economists] end up depicting is a parody, purged of all that is dark and destructive, its warlike competition reduced to a fairy ballet." Elsewhere Shaikh emphasizes, "All the basic tropes of orthodox economics—perfect competition, rational expectations, perfect knowledge of the consumer, no interactions among consumers or firms directly, general equilibrium, optimality, efficiency—all of these concepts are based on this notion of the representation of capitalism as ideal."

The replacement of the concept of real competition with that of perfect competition also compromises the understanding of the process of capital concentration. In fact, according to conventional theory, monopolies and oligopolies are terrible exceptions, a distortion of the market, to be fought against because they contradict the logic of harmonious competition leading to perfect equilibrium. On the contrary, a critical lens allows us to observe that, far from being "a break" with competition, monopolies are precisely its expression in action. As Shaikh reminds us, monopoly is not the antithesis of the market but the result of its dynamics.

The critical economist is not particularly concerned with judging the intentions of individual capitalists (whether they are greedy or selfless, whether they care about the environment and their workers, etc., is beside the point). Our perspective is not moralistic nor individualistic but political and systemic, a view that is both more powerful in terms of explanation and stronger in terms of practical action. We want to understand the role played by different classes in shaping a system of which they are both architects and prisoners. This does not mean embracing a crude determinism or absolving ourselves as passive elements in a system that operates on its own. On the contrary, we must consider ourselves as builders of a network of oppression that defines our economic system and avoid deluding ourselves: replacing Antonio Filosa, the CEO of Stellantis, with Shawn Fain, the head of the United Auto Workers, will not be enough to abolish exploitation as the basis of our society. Indeed, once we chose to organize the production and distribution of our material conditions through the competition of private producers that operate to increase profits and relate to one another via monetary transactions, the pressure to cut the costs of production took primacy over all else.

The particular logic that governs our economic system and the forces that compel and restrain our behaviors are not inevitable. The capital order, held with such reverence by so many neoclassical economists and buoyed by the apparent rigor of mathematics, is actually the result of fragile political balances.

2.

THE LOGIC OF AUSTERITY

The capital order has an essentially relational, and thus political, nature. Far from being a self-sustaining given, it is a choice that requires constant life support. A pseudo-moral principle and economic policy known as austerity has been perfected over time as a means to safeguard capitalism and weaken the possibility that any alternative economic system might emerge. Austerity consists of a set of economic policies implemented by governmental institutions that cut across party lines. Often, it is paradoxically the self-styled left that leverages austerity.

Much economic research has established that austerity has almost never worked as promised, neither stimulating growth nor reducing debt. So why does it continue to be the preferred course of action for governments? We cannot simply attribute its structural presence to the stupidity or corruption of those in government. The true measure of austerity's effectiveness is its ability to impose and reinforce a class structure, the very order that underpins economic growth. In this sense, austerity has never been an irrational calculation.

If you ask most experts for a definition of austerity, they will say it is economic policies that involve cutting public spending and raising taxes. Here lies the first trap: economists like to measure the aggregate, the sum total, the whole. These experts talk about the US, the French, and the Brazilian economies as cohesive national entities. But this view overlooks how public money is spent differently across economic classes. If we examine the aggregate spending of the American state, we won't see any trace of austerity. In fact, the state is spending heavily, especially to secure shareholder profit with public handouts to private entities in the military-industrial complex, prison management, and financial sectors. For example, the Biden administration's "Bidenomics" had the state take on debt to de-risk and effectively subsidize asset managers investing in the green transition and spend over $22 billion in military aid to Israel between 2023 and 2024, guaranteeing business for more than fifty multinational companies involved in the genocide in Gaza. Total public spending is not falling. Fiscal austerity is not simply about *whether* the state is spending, but rather about *where* the state is spending or, better yet, *for whom*.

In 2022, the official rate of child poverty more than doubled in the US, with 5.2 million more children living in poverty. This followed a congressional decision to end emergency COVID-19 relief support with cuts in the child tax credit, food subsidies, and unemployment insurance. If the American state, like most states worldwide, increases military spending or rescues banks and supports private businesses, while simultaneously cutting welfare spending, it is structurally transferring resources from the majority of citizens who live off their wages to the 1 percent who live on gains from capital ownership, such as dividends, rents, and interest. Austerity is not about spending less but about spending in favor of the economic and financial elite and to the detriment of the majority of the population. We struggle to afford basic medical treatment, find secure affordable housing, and send our children to adequately funded schools. Though social expenditures are slashed, for the capitalist class the message that "there's no money" doesn't apply. The American state bought nearly $50 billion in arms from Lockheed Martin in 2023 alone. In fact, Lockheed Martin and BlackRock overflow with our tax money. Meanwhile, European countries sacrifice social spending on the altar of their new NATO defense spending target of five percent of GDP.

These austerity maneuvers are not merely technical decisions; they are profoundly political choices. Austerity achieves a crucial goal: it increases workers' dependence on the market. As the state dismantles health care, education, social housing, transportation, and public services, we must worry about having money in our pockets to meet our basic needs. If we want to secure a good education for our children, adequate medical treatment, a roof to live under, and the right to transportation, we are increasingly tied to the need to have sufficient money, which most of us can obtain in only one way: by selling our capacity to work in exchange for a wage. If we barely have the energy to make it to the end of the month, how can we find the strength to participate in any collective initiative toward alternative economic structures or even just protect our rights?

The same principle applies to the other side of the fiscal austerity coin, state revenues: it is not about *whether* the state increases taxes, but about *whom* it increases taxes *for*. Today, most governments enact regressive tax reforms, cutting taxes for those with capital income (and providing generous tax loopholes) while increasing taxes for those with labor income, who have little room for evasion given that they are taxed directly from their paychecks. In the US, people who earn income from wages are taxed disproportionately more than those who earn income through capital gains—most of which, of course, are earned by the rich.

In 2019, the top 1 percent of households accounted for 75 percent of all capital gains in the US, and the top 0.1 percent earned nearly half of all capital gains income, a trend that has only intensified in the last few years. Moreover, while sales taxes, excise taxes (on fuel), and taxes on alcohol—which we all pay equally regardless of income—are growing in most American states, taxes on the top income brackets are declining (from 92 percent in 1953 to 37 percent in 2023) as are federal corporate taxes (from 35 percent to 21 percent in 2017).

Thus, we get bizarre scenarios where, in a corporation like the Walt Disney Company, a custodian would have to work two thousand years to make as much as the CEO does in one year, and shareholders pay far less in taxes than the workers who generate the corporation's surplus. Walt Disney is certainly not a uniquely rotten apple; such gross inequalities are found throughout the economy. In 2018, corporations that paid zero dollars in federal income tax included all the big names: IBM, Starbucks, Netflix, Delta, Chevron, GM, and Amazon. In 2020, Nike, HP, and FedEx were granted the same exemption. Another glaring example is the elimination of the inheritance tax. In the United States, for example, thanks to the mechanism of an annuity trust, multimillionaires can pass on their wealth to the next generations tax-free.

In the US, as elsewhere, cuts in investors' taxes are marketed with the message that these measures will incentivize those who run our economy to invest and increase jobs. But historical evidence speaks clearly: these corporate giveaways benefit only the superrich. For example, thanks to the Trump tax cut of 2017, AT&T gained a tax windfall of $21 billion, yet eliminated 23,328 jobs in the two years following.

You may find these scenarios paradoxical or even a reflection of the failure of our economic policies. I don't blame you. What I want to stress, however, is that these results are *not* a failure for the logic of our economic system. The result of regressive taxation is the same as that of cuts to social spending: the confiscation of the working peoples' resources increases their economic vulnerability, their precariousness, and dependence on the market. These are definitely problems for us but not for the system, because securing market dependence means securing the foundations of the capital order.

We can dismiss the common trope by which austerity policies are conceived as a zero-sum game between the state and the market. Austerity capitalism does not mean less state intervention; it means a state that constantly plays an active role in fortifying the market by expropriating resources from the many to favor the few.

Fiscal austerity, such as defunding social services and cutting taxes on the rich, is often implemented alongside monetary policies, particularly by increasing interest rates, which swells the incomes of capital owners—those same individuals whom the state chooses not to tax but instead borrows from, paying them interest.

Interest rate hikes, thanks to monetary austerity, are good news for creditors but bad news for families who depend on loans for their daily survival and who will find themselves paying higher mortgages and amassing more credit card debt. Working families are not just hit as consumers; they are hit harder as workers. First, the higher cost of money increases government borrowing expenses for social services, which will therefore be cut. Second, monetary austerity directly impacts the labor market. The high cost of money, in fact, slows down the economy: as employers reduce spending, fewer job opportunities and higher unemployment undermine the bargaining power of workers. Monetary austerity determined the US Federal Reserve's agenda in 2022 and 2023 and cost American workers 1.2 million job openings between May 2023 and May 2024 alone.

The wave of monetary austerity that broke in 2022 was preceded by more than a decade of low interest rates. This did not enrich workers. As Janet Yellen reminded us, "Interest rates can be low only when workers are weak." Easy money and forms of quantitative easing that immediately secured the assets of large corporations were politically compatible with the capital order because of previous waves of austerity. At the end of the 1970s, when workers' organizations were strong, Fed Chairman Paul Volcker began raising interest rates, which would peak at 20 percent in the early 1980s. These decisions caused an economic recession in the US and many parts of the world, with American unemployment rising to 10 percent, breaking the back of workers at a moment of historical mobilization for higher wages and anti-capitalist alternatives. If you, as a worker, fear losing your job and, with it, the ability to pay for medical care, you become more controllable. If job opportunities are scarce, wages decrease. The risk of spiraling an economy into a recession is a short-term cost for capital accumulation: securing workers' subordination and a healthy rate of exploitation come first.

Industrial austerity shows up in the direct intervention of the state in the labor market, through privatizing, dismantling labor rights, and weakening unions. As the state transfers industries to private companies, it makes the labor market precarious and weakens workers.

This is the austerity trinity of fiscal, monetary, and industrial pressures. They have little to do with technicalities like balancing the budget and much to do with maintaining a society of few winners and many losers, increasingly isolated and trapped in material conditions that prevent them from carving out time and space to imagine a different social model.

The economic institutions in charge, from countries' central banks and treasuries to the International Monetary Fund, serve the primary purpose of "stabilizing" our economy. A close reading of history shows that to achieve such stabilization, labor relations must be shaped against workers so that they have no alternative but to accept a subordinate role in the production process. The toolbox of macroeconomic management—social expenditure cuts, regressive taxation, interest rate hikes, privatization—is based on the sacrifice of working people. Again, this goal takes precedence over all others, even at the cost of a temporary economic recession or greater debt. Indeed, it is easy to unmask the political priorities at stake when considering, for example, the cost to American citizens of not taxing the rich. According to the US Treasury, taxing capital gains at death instead of allowing them to be passed on untaxed would raise over $400 billion for the country over the next decade, almost exclusively from the wealthiest 1 percent. In 2023 the federal government spent less than a third of this amount on nutrition assistance programs, including food stamps. The systematic defunding of the Internal Revenue Service is another emblematic case in point. The firing of public employees under the pretext of depleting state coffers has ironically cost an estimated $7.5 trillion in over a decade, nearly 4.5 times the 2023 fiscal year deficit. Austerity capitalism is expensive.

Trump's "One Big Beautiful Bill," enacted July 4, 2025, captures the violent arithmetic of austerity: Over the next decade, historic cuts to the social safety net will bankroll a staggering expansion of military and border-control spending. Nearly $200 billion stripped from food assistance—likely pushing more than two million poor Americans toward hunger—will now finance detention centers, border surveillance, and next-generation military tech, securing profits for private shareholders. More than $500 billion carved out of Medicaid will deprive millions of health care coverage, even as those earning over $1 million a year enjoy a collective $114 billion tax break in 2027 alone. And far from reducing the national deficit, the bill is projected to swell it by more than $4 trillion in a decade—making it, in the words of the Democratic House Budget Committee, "one of the most expensive laws in American history." Once again, austerity is not about taming debt; it is about deepening market dependence and tightening the grip of the capital order.

It's time to stop buying into the idea that, within a capitalist society, it makes sense to discuss economic policies according to the criterion of "right" and "wrong" for an elusive common good. Our economic machinery is structured not to meet the needs of ordinary people but to increase the rents and profits of the few capital holders. Economic policies cater to these priorities. What critics point to as "problems" of the system—poverty, inequality, and unemployment—are actually its precise "solutions."

Austerity isn't something abstract: we experience it every day. Even if we can't define it, we actually know it very well. It has a disruptive impact on our lives and determines their quality: what we eat, where we live, the air we breathe. In the UK, a country that has punished its citizens with social spending cuts since 2009, following the government's intervention to enrich those same bankers whose risky bets had brought misery to the majority, the average life expectancy has decreased. In the United States, tormented by structural austerity, life expectancy is lower than that of any other Western country, and wealthy male citizens have a life expectancy that is fifteen years higher than the poorest.

The vital role of austerity becomes glaringly apparent when the economic system enters a crisis. True crises of capitalism, far more than mere slowdowns in economic growth, are moments when the majority questions the pillars of our economy: private ownership of the means of production and wage labor. In the aftermath of the Great War, significant portions of the population in countries such as Britain and Italy were embracing concrete institutional transformations. What halted the transition toward greater economic democracy was an expert-driven campaign to code austerity as an objective resolution to the crisis of capitalism.

History reveals that austerity is not merely an aberration of the neoliberal turn in the 1970s, as is often believed. Rather, it is a structural component of our economic system. While governments tend to pass austerity policies to counter worker protests during times of labor upheaval, it remains a fixed rule of all governments within a capitalist system.

A History of Coercion

We see the coercive nature of fiscal, monetary, and industrial austerity at the beginning of the twentieth century, after World War I, alongside the rise of fascism, and in today's policies.

Investigating what happened a century ago, when austerity emerged to discipline workers across Europe, allows us to dig deeper into its current logic and dismantle those misunderstandings that silence dissent and resistance. The narrative that follows—resulting from extensive archival research—is crucial for exposing the "false opposition" between political parties of different colors that confront each other in public debate.

The Great War from 1914 to 1918 triggered arguably the most severe crisis capitalism has ever experienced. Extraordinary economic challenges posed by war mobilization pushed governments to intervene in a way that shook the pillars of capitalism. As soon as hopes for a swift resolution of the armed conflict vanished, governments found themselves facing an industrial war. Increasing production became essential for military victory, and the home front took on a decisive strategic importance. The challenge was daunting: how to boost production to have enough raw materials, weapons, arsenals, technology, and food to win against the enemy while much of the working population was fighting at the front. In the case of Great Britain, almost six million men were enlisted in the army, accounting for more than a third of the available male workforce.

The governing elites entered the war firmly believing in the power of what eighteenth-century Scottish economist Adam Smith called the "invisible hand": private business and the law of supply and demand were enough to guarantee the most efficient production results. But the elites' faith was soon tested. The increase in demand for war necessities raised prices but not productivity. While society suffered from food shortages and inflation, private business channeled resources into more profitable sectors, such as luxury goods and exports.

The case of the British naval sector illustrates a general pattern. As the War Cabinet reported to Parliament, "If shipping failed, we could neither continue in the war nor maintain our population." Soon, the conflict between public needs and private interests plainly surfaced: selling British ships abroad was extremely profitable. By February 1917, private shipowners had sold ships to rival nations at such a rate that there were not even enough vessels to import the essential goods for a nation at war. As Sir Leo George Chiozza Money, the parliamentary secretary to the British Ministry of Shipping, wrote, it was only when the state found itself "on the edge of the abyss" that it abandoned the notion of "doctrinaire individualism."

Faced with a choice between victory or defeat, the governments of the warring countries introduced unprecedented economic practices. The words of Edward M. H. Lloyd, a civil servant in the British War Ministry, summarized this shift: "National organization and centralized control were found to be more effective than high prices and laissez-faire in stimulating supply." Comprehensive state intervention was underway. As early as 1915, the Italian economist Riccardo Bachi wrote, "The State, as a war entrepreneur, has become the center, the pivot, the engine of the entire economy."

The political scope of these upheavals was terrifying. Paradoxically, to promote capital accumulation, the state intervened with maneuvers so extraordinary that they overturned the social consensus on which the system rested: the idea that it was a spontaneous, untouchable, and natural order. At that critical juncture, the state opened economic analysis to political discussion. Policies cementing private ownership of the means of production and wage relations were now debatable.

The British and Italian governments, among those of other

nations, took control of industrial and agricultural production. Both endowed themselves with broad powers, including the requisition of goods and lands; they also set limits on private profits. While wartime collectivism opened the bureaucrats' imagination to forms of nationalization, the states' interventions to regulate the labor market had even more politically disruptive consequences. In those years, workers experienced firsthand the impact of state initiatives aimed at dismantling their bargaining power.

World War I shifted the power relations between capital and labor. Just as wartime production was increasing, conscription and voluntary enlistment depleted the reserve army of labor. If this were left to the dynamics of competition to attract workers, capitalists would have had to bid up wages to levels that were incompatible with "national goals" of intensified capital accumulation. At that point, the state had to intervene. Increasing productivity primarily meant disciplining the workers.

The Italian government went so far as to militarize the workforce. This meant that when a firm was declared "auxiliary," all personnel, from senior technicians to laborers, including women, the elderly, and children, fell under military jurisdiction. This gave rise to the phenomenon of "factory barracks," as labor leader Bruno Buozzi called them. Indeed, workers were officially equated with soldiers: they had to submit to mandatory work and adhere to a strict work regimen enforced by the military. Any unauthorized absence was considered insubordination, obstructionism, and sabotage and severely punished. By the end of the war, 50 percent of Italian workers had faced sanctions.

The state's role as disciplinarian altered the specific characteristics of capitalism as a socioeconomic system. Instead of bosses, it was now governments implementing the harshest techniques to increase the rate of exploitation. They prevented workers from accepting better-paid jobs, kept wages low, and extended the working day by making overtime mandatory. The Italian government froze wages at prewar levels and even suspended the prohibition on night work for women and children in most cases. All these processes made capitalist exploitation—once impersonal—overtly political, exposing it to public scrutiny and resistance. The state thus triggered an unexpected and potentially fatal crisis for the economic system it was paradoxically trying to protect.

The crisis of capitalism stemmed from the actions of men and women who firmly believed in a different world and personally dedicated themselves to realizing it. The war had demonstrated that production relations were not set in stone and could therefore be changed, not only to favor capital—as the capitalist state had done—but also to build a more humane society that centered on the satisfaction and well-being of those who had been indispensable during the conflict. No matter how much the capitalist class tried to deny it, there would have been no military victory without the workers who were exploited in the factories and massacred on the front lines. The most creative political thinkers of the period immediately following World War I were able to build workers' awareness and then propose ideas of profound social transformation. Powerful economic systems could be invented, revised, and transformed by people. There was nothing natural or immutable about the economic system they had grown up in. Capitalist oppression could be overthrown through struggle.

It is difficult to do justice to the enormous wealth of social experiments that were realized in the immediate postwar period, such as in Italy during the so-called Red Biennium. Scholars have preferred to spill ink on the following decade, beginning with the crisis of 1929, when workers had already lost their bargaining power and democratic alternatives to capitalism had faded. But between 1918 and 1920, workers were politically stronger than ever before.

These battles were fought in the very heart of capitalism, in Western European countries. The popular imagination in the West was undoubtedly ignited by the radical changes in Eastern Europe, from Russia to Hungary, where workers had succeeded in toppling ancient authoritarian and semifeudal regimes. The writings of the Italian politician Pietro Nenni convey the sense of excitement:

> The fall of the Hohenzollern in Germany, the dissolution of the Habsburg empire and the flight of its last emperor, the Spartacist movements in Berlin, the Bolshevik revolution in Hungary, the Soviet in Bavaria ... fired the imaginations and inspired the hope that the old world was on the point of crumbling and that humanity was on the verge of a new era of a new social order.

This "new social order" took on multiple faces, from reformists to the more radicals.

Let's start with the "reconstructionists," composed of an enlightened elite of bureaucrats, public intellectuals, and union representatives who, in their effort to use the redistributive power of the state to save capitalism, inadvertently undermined its foundations.

Reconstructionists launched a significant attack on economic orthodoxy, which had controlled and defined the political decisions of states for more than a century. For the Italian politician Michele Pietravalle, the time had come to revise "material and moral values, and even to rethink, shake, break, knock down constitutions and institutions that once appeared as fundamental and sacred." The war, British journalist John Hammond wrote in 1918, "had emancipated and widened our imaginations" since it "removed the word 'impossible' from the language of politics" and "destroyed the superstition of the iron law which has checked and hampered all our hopes."

Reconstructionists held that political and social issues came before economic priorities. They argued that monetary resources would be sufficient to achieve the political objectives of the state, regardless of their cost. In Great Britain, Minister of Transport Eric Geddes voiced a popular view in his report to the cabinet on February 25, 1919: "You must be prepared to spend money on after-the-war problems as you did on during-the-war problems. That [money] must be found and added to our debt if necessary." Minister for Reconstruction Christopher Addison, who campaigned for the adoption of urgent social reforms, was in agreement: "It would be no defense to say that vital proposals were not enacted for want of money. *Nobody will believe it.*"

These were not just words; governments implemented mandatory health insurance, unemployment insurance, and the right to primary education. In Britain, for example, the Ministry of Reconstruction, which many Italian reformists looked to as a model, established visionary committees. The women's subcommittee for housing, composed entirely of women, proposed experiments in "community living." It created gardens, playgrounds, and social centers, believing that "full attention should be given to the organisation of the resources available for social and intellectual development." A section of the report, titled "Communal Holiday Homes," confronted "the difficulty experienced by working women in obtaining a real rest and holiday." The plan envisaged "(1) Houses in which mothers could, without anxiety, leave their young children . . . [and] (2) Large houses in seaside or country places to which groups of working people might go for a holiday."

The Adult Education Committee in Britain manifested the spirit of the time, following an ideal still to be realized: "Adult education is a permanent national necessity, an inseparable aspect of citizenship, and therefore should be both universal and lifelong." It advocated for education that was "systematic," "continuous," and "social" as a "duty of the community," which would satisfy workers' "appetite for knowledge," and overcome "work without thought."

During the same years, the Turin-based magazine *L'Ordine nuovo* (The new order), founded in May 1919 by young political leaders and intellectuals Antonio Gramsci and Palmiro Togliatti and their comrades, found its lifeblood in the city's workers' councils and carried its ideas to their revolutionary consequences. Mobilizations during the Red Biennium sought to establish democratic control of production.

The "strikomania" that spread across Italy and Great Britain in 1919 drove an unusually large number of workers to put down tools and to fight for fewer working hours and higher wages. As an official British communiqué explained, workers were "no longer prepared to acquiesce in a system in which their labour is bought and sold as a commodity in the labour market," and demanded to be treated "not as 'hands' or part of the factory equipment" but "as human beings with a right to use their abilities by hand and brain in the service not of the few but of the whole community."

In Italy, the desire for popular self-governance spread rapidly through factories and the countryside. While industrial workers in northern Italy fought for control over the means of production, more than three hundred thousand agricultural workers staged a fifty-day strike across vast areas of Piedmont and Lombardy, holding many citywide assemblies. These workers occupied land and collectively managed agriculture through self-governed institutions, including councils to deliberate on production, employment offices to coordinate labor, and production cooperatives to supply fertilizers and machinery. They often succeeded in gaining state recognition for these institutions. Similar successes were realized by workers in the manufacturing sector. The primary goals of the Red Biennium were to abolish the exploitative wage relationship in favor of horizontal participation in production and to abolish production for profit in favor of production for need.

Factory councils became popular in Scotland's Clydeside region and reached their peak in Italy in the summer of 1920 with the occupation of factories. During this time, workers managed production autonomously for over a month. Italian Prime Minister Giovanni Giolitti had to admit the impossibility of the state intervening in defense of private capital due to the extreme deployment of forces that such a task would have required.

Similarly, the directors of the main banks, for example Banca Commerciale, were forced to assure the metalworkers' union that they would remain neutral, asking for leniency in case of a revolutionary outcome. Even Benito Mussolini, leader of the movement Fasci Italiani di Combattimento (Italian Fasci of Combat, later to become a party), took care to communicate his solidarity with the occupiers, while Fiat owner Giovanni Agnelli, in 1920, during the days of the factory occupation, officially proposed to transform the entire company into a cooperative.

Particularly inspiring is the way political-cultural projects provided lifeblood to the movement in those years. The weekly *L'Ordine nuovo* was a hub of political reflection that contributed to the deep conviction that no true social revolution is possible without a revolution in the way we understand society. Gramsci named this mutually reinforcing connection between theory and collective action "praxis." As a young philosophy student, he had experienced the power of human activity to transform reality and produce history during his participation in the workers' councils of Turin. The intellectual insights gained from his political engagement became the guiding intuition of his famous *Prison Notebooks*, written during the years of his detention by the fascist regime.

Until the Red Biennium, knowledge had been filtered from

the top down to ensure passive consent to the current system. However, Gramsci and his comrades now understood that emancipatory knowledge had to emerge from collective organizing in the workplace and could thus support action from the bottom up. They learned this at the factory councils, which were born as informal committees representing workers during the Great War. These councils became the institutional basis for a new liberating force. They were true schools for the people and signaled the end of the separation between economics and politics. Decisions regarding production were reappropriated by the workers, who realized that making collective economic choices required experimenting with novel constitutional structures capable of ensuring genuine democratic participation. Unlike our current political systems, where elected officials often exercise unchecked discretion and align with powerful interests, the representatives within the various levels of the councils were subject to recall by their base, rotated every six months, and required "to announce frequent referenda in their departments on social and technical questions and hold frequent assemblies." As "absolutely original institutions" of the proletariat, the councils functioned as nuclei of a new state—one in which people were not alienated from political life but actively engaged in it on a daily basis. The democratic organization of economic decision-making built novel skills and prepared workers for a new society.

Merging politics into our understanding of economics is how we create real democracy. It requires recognizing how a worker can have conscious agency as a creator of value. While today capitalism and traditional economic models render us powerless by treating us as interchangeable pieces in a production process we do not control, what *L'Ordine nuovo* emphasized was the collective strength of workers as indispensable to society.

The affirmation of workers' agency as self-governing producers, the union of economics and politics, and the meshing of theory and practice were steps toward emancipation. However, as Gramsci observed, either popular organizations manage to go beyond capitalist relations or the ruling class will find a way to reimpose its dominance.

Beginning in 1922, Mussolini's fascist regime imposed austerity policies that enabled the restoration of old power relations. It implemented fiscal austerity by systematically dismantling the popular postwar gains, severely cutting welfare spending, and abolishing inheritance and super-profit taxes, while simultaneously increasing taxes on workers. Monetary and industrial austerity followed: the fascist government raised interest rates and banned unions and strikes, using legal force to suppress wages and consolidate control. To establish these policies, Il Duce astutely surrounded himself with economists who reestablished the barrier between the economic and the political that workers had dared to break.

This counteroffensive based on austerity policies still affects our lives today. The first international economics conferences in Brussels (1920) and Genoa (1922) were hotbeds for developing an antiworker project that was both intelligent and ruthless. The experts in economics and finance gathered to forge the code of austerity and deceive the public into believing that any alternative to the capital order was impossible. At a time when wartime collectivism had challenged the efficiency of the market in mediating production and distribution, these economists had to stand firm and unite in defending its idealization. Just when class conflict seemed to reach a point of no return, they denied its very existence by reverting to "classless" economic models that quietly subordinated workers. They did not mince words. Citizens who expected a reward for their wartime sacrifices had to think again: the "prize" of reconstruction would not be democratic control of industry or a new and advanced welfare system but, as the British investment banker R. H. Brand put it, the "hard truth" of "labour and suffering."

Austerity had a precise purpose: to defend capitalism from its enemies. And it responded to an iron logic: to attribute economic problems—debt and inflation—to those enemies. The motto coined in Brussels and Genoa, "Work more, consume less," pointed its accusing finger at the workers. What the experts gathered at the two conferences knew for sure was that the logic of capitalism would not recover without forceful political intervention by the state, which would weaken the workers by transferring resources from the many to the few. Here lies the quintessential achievement of macroeconomics as it has long been practiced, modifying and disciplining citizens' behavior through fiscal and monetary policy.

The economists of the time certainly did not view themselves as agents of repression. Rather, they considered austerity reforms as products of an objective reality, which could not be questioned. The state and its representatives implemented a powerful strategy that took on two faces—consent and coercion—and was carried out across Europe.

Economics professors played a pivotal role during the early

years of Mussolini's government. In the 1920s, a strong alliance formed among some leading academics. Two were openly fascist and two were liberals. They believed the workers' social alternatives were leading the nation toward moral and economic decline and so perfected the weapon of austerity against them. Professor Maffeo Pantaleoni snarked:

> Thanks to Bolshevism, the modesty in the standard of living that characterized Italians has vanished. It has disappeared in both the working class and the peasantry. It is disgusting to witness the masses of workers that are drunk in all our cities. . . . The notable increase of wages was not accompanied by greater civilization.

These cruel words came from the pen of someone who is still remembered as one of the most important economists of all time and is a founding father of the economic theory that is still dominant today, the "neoclassical paradigm." Pantaleoni's *Principles of Pure Economics*, translated into English in 1898, represented a methodological turning point for economic studies, training generations of students. His international fame secured him a seat at the Brussels conference of 1920. A committed member of the Fascist Party and a senator since 1923, Pantaleoni worked strenuously in the role of first technical adviser to his student Alberto De' Stefani, who in 1922 became the minister of finance and treasury of the fascist government.

A professor of economics with tenures in Padua, Venice, and Rome, De' Stefani was elected among the first deputies of the Fascist Party as early as 1921. After becoming finance minister, he called to his side Professor Umberto Ricci, whom Mussolini had recruited to serve his government. Unlike his two colleagues, Ricci was not a fascist but a true liberal who aligned with the fourth member of the austerity squad, Professor Luigi Einaudi, in believing that Mussolini was the right man at the right time to put an end to the absurd demands of the workers. To understand Einaudi's support of fascist economic policy, it is enough to read one of his numerous articles in *The Economist*, for which he was a correspondent:

> When the worst happened, in September last, and the occupation of factories by armed workers and the institution of Soviets in factories seemed to point to an imminent Communist revolution in Italy, and the government declared its impotence to use the armed force for the enforcement of the law, a sudden revolution took place. Youths of the middle class, returned men and officers, in indignation grouped themselves into "fasci." . . . The communists are everywhere defeated. . . . This renewed feeling of hope in the future of our country is not the least important cause of the better tone in foreign exchanges.

The four distinguished academics saw fascism as a turning point driven by a "set of politicians: young, energetic, full of vigor and patriotism." On October 28, 1922, Einaudi wrote:

> The important question is, what is the economic platform of the new party? Signor Mussolini, the chief, is not an economist. Passionate and full of vigor, he is able to com-

mit his party to headlong plunges into unknown seas. For the moment, he has uttered at Naples only one economic sentence: "Italy needs at the helm a man capable of saying no to all requests of new expenditure." So far, so good. . . . Public opinion was seriously and gravely warned of the necessity of putting an end to the increase in public expenditure, and of reducing even useful expenses. . . . Will the new Party have the will and the power to redress the awkward financial situation of the State?

In the *Corriere della sera* just a few days earlier, Einaudi had praised the economic program of the National Fascist Party, presented by De' Stefani at the Naples congress that same month: "We ardently desire a party, and be it the Fascist one if the others can't do better, who can use the appropriate means to reach the objective of the spiritual and economic grandeur of our homeland [patria]."

"Grandeur of our homeland" really means capitalist accumulation, to which everything had to be sacrificed. As the economic programs developed, the ideological differences between the two fascist professors and the two liberals disappeared, blended into a tacitly shared coercive design. Once in office, in January 1922, De' Stefani wrote to his "illustrious friend" Einaudi extolling their unity of purpose:

> When my young and bold comrades ask me how to develop a Fascist mentality, also in the technical field of social, economic and financial problems, I direct them to the works of four great Italian Fascists, who are non-militant and

without a party card: Vilfredo Pareto, Maffeo Pantaleoni, Umberto Ricci and "last but not the least" Luigi Einaudi, whom I plead my comrades to forgive if he propagandizes for Fascism on the columns of the *Corriere della sera*.

The fascist mindset was perfectly aligned with that of the capitalist economists. They quickly understood that the regime would set the conditions to bring their ideal economic models to fruition, ultimately supporting the construction of an all but impregnable capitalist society.

Pure Economics

One must consider both the neoclassical economists' theoretical writings and newspaper contributions to fully understand the coherence of the austerity project. The professors' public commentary unveils the classism that imbues their economic essays, which technical language otherwise masks. The urgency to discipline workers was, in fact, dictated by a scientific calculation. In turn, the scientific aura helped vindicate austerity policies.

The new theoretical paradigm of "pure economics" was not yet dominant, especially in Italy, where the economic tradition was historical rather than mathematical. De' Stefani and Ricci hailed Pantaleoni as "an Archangel with a flaming sword" who was fighting against all other schools of economic thought to spread a "theoretical part of economic science, a nucleus of doctrines, that are independent of opinions, as well as of ethical, political and religious predilections. Something akin

THE LOGIC OF AUSTERITY   83

to physics and mathematics . . . an exact science definable as 'pure economics.'"

The success of this mental straitjacket depended on its ability to appear impartial, which guaranteed the economist undisputed authority. He deserved to be equated with a scientist capable of dispensing objective and incontrovertible truths. As Ricci explained, "The socialist and the protectionist are to the economist as the astrologer is to the astronomer, the alchemist to the chemist, the charlatan to the doctor." These economists meticulously endeavored to garner unanimous consensus for austerity and to consecrate economists as an exclusive circle holding positive knowledge about all economic phenomena.

De' Stefani described his excitement when, stumbling upon Pantaleoni's *Principii* and Pareto's *Cours d'économie* in a bookstore, he discovered pure economics:

> I was seduced by those analyses in which utility and harm, pleasure and pain, and the more complex facts of the economic order were conducted through calculus formulae and described through graphical representations. . . . Equilibria became points of intersection of curve systems and numbers solving systems of equations. The soul was soothed by these formal truths.

As the rigor of arithmetic soothed the economist, quantitative methods bolstered his claims to objectivity. If numbers do not lie, neither can pure economics, which is entirely built on mathematical models.

The insistence on objectivity was so relentless that it even manifested in the change of the discipline's name, from political economy to pure economics. This purity derived from a savvy focus on a narrow range of elements: the economist dealt only with individual decisions of hypothetical rational beings, from which unassailable theorems could be deduced. Many economists do not even discuss human beings but a caricature of them, *Homo economicus*—the rational agent driven by self-interest—and his decisions aimed at maximizing utility.

At the same time, this "purity" sweeps away all historical institutions of the real economic world, forbidding questions about what should and shouldn't be private property and how class relations need to be addressed. Most important, pure economics presumes eternal capitalism by avoiding the use of the term altogether. By elevating economics to a pseudoscientific discipline, the experts carried out a forced and methodical separation of the economic sphere of society from the political one. One might think that this separation would make economics a mere intellectual exercise. Ironically, it was this very separation that justified coercive intervention into society's behavior.

These experts felt a strong urge to shape people's lives in order to comply with their transcendent discoveries. Ricci believed theoretical constructions should "be deemed not merely a luxury of the intellect, but necessary to explain and predict events, and essential to tame men."

Blessed with unbiased knowledge, the pure economist has a moral duty to show citizens where they have gone wrong and correct them. Here lies the key to understanding technocracy, which etymologically means "power of the expert."

After the war, however, the opposition to the experts' vision was evident. Ricci was aware that if the "contemplation" of the "divine science" was "the privilege of the few," it was also true that this science "does not always appear beautiful, true and good to the profane public." Hence his regret: "By proclaiming the principle of universal taxation, the shutting down of redundant employees and of useless public works, the economist surely does not make friends."

The profound political ambitions of these supposedly apolitical economists become evident when they discuss the "authentic essence" of the world. In 1920, in the pages of *Corriere della sera*, Einaudi led a polemic against Marxist ideas circulating in Italy: "Why should a capitalist profit only because the machine is his? Why shall he live without doing anything? Is it not obvious that his profit comes from the exploitation of someone else's labour?" he asked sarcastically, and continued: "This is the celebrated and vulgar sophism of Karl Marx's *Capital*.... But it is enough to ask: how much would be produced if the savers did not produce capital? The answer: nothing. Without capital, labour produces zero."

De' Stefani offered an analogous explanation to his students: "Capitalism is the phenomenon of a class that lives on the specific productivity of capital, it depends on the right of property and heredity, not on a subtraction at the expense of the workers." It was, he specified, "a result of savings and conservation, useful actually to the very working classes."

While Gramsci and the revolutionary workers used lived economic knowledge to expose the reality of capitalism as a system based on exploitation, the pure economists defended models that depicted a reality in which capital, not labor, was the engine of the economic machine. Capital was understood not as a social relationship but as a commodity generated by the savings of those who deserved to be at the top of the pyramid.

The pure economists went even further. According to their impartial science, social hierarchies were not only natural but also just, because a person's class was a result of individual choices. The theoretical assumption is that in a society governed by the market, anyone capable of maintaining virtuous economic behavior can succeed. This is the fairy tale of meritocracy.

Ricci believed that economic success couldn't be achieved by everyone, not because of the inherent injustice of the economic system but because of the small number of virtuous citizens in society. The capacity to save was a talent reserved for only a few. Ricci wrote, "Amongst the tools with which man can elevate himself in the scale of civilization, individual abstinence is both the most effective and least widespread."

Pantaleoni drew on the lexicon of evolutionary science to define the virtue of entrepreneurs, speaking of their capacity to preserve the species through behavior that centers on rational self-interest: "[They] realise almost perfectly the type of the *homo economicus*, and who therefore know, and take advantage, of every opportunity that presents itself of earning a profit."

If the few deserve the position of economic privilege they occupy, everyone else should thank them for the collective "prosperity" they create. Far from being the outcome of unpaid labor, capital as described in the models of pure economists is the result of individuals' capacity to save and invest, on which the well-being of everyone else depends. It was therefore advantageous for all, and beneficial for the workers themselves, that "the direction of the labour of the masses" would rest once again "in the hands of the men of talent and personality whom selection makes into entrepreneurs."

This worldview seduces many of us daily, to the point where we respect those at the top of the pyramid and feel at least somewhat annoyed by those who fail to succeed—including our own children. As Pantaleoni remarked: "The classes with lower incomes are significantly deficient in comparison to others, so much so that this deficiency is the cause of their lower income, and not that the lower income is the cause of the deficiency."

Injustice lay in the disorder that economics professors saw in society after World War I, where the unworthy had gained too much and had the audacity to demand more. Whether it was their classism fueling economic theory or vice versa doesn't matter. What does is that the two aspects reinforced each other, creating a sense of repugnance toward the "lazy," which grew into the disgust that many today display toward those who receive welfare and other state subsidies. Even many poor workers agree with these economists' thesis.

In the summer of 2021, I handed out flyers in the markets of working-class neighborhoods in Turin, Italy, to help a local independent party, and I often talked with passersby. Many were indignant about the economy, but they did not direct their anger toward the top 1 percent of the population, who paid insignificant taxes, or the Italian billionaires, whose numbers had tripled in the past ten years. Instead, they directed their anger toward the "cheaters," who benefited from the meager basic income of 400 euros (about $470) a month. Note that 46 percent of these cheaters actually worked but did not make enough to survive; they fell into the growing category of the working poor. In 2023, Giorgia Meloni's government took advantage of the dominant narrative and eliminated the subsidy: 250,000 Italian families were notified via text of the reform that would relapse them below the poverty line. Popular reaction to such a war against the poor was almost nonexistent.

A hundred years ago, this toxic narrative had not yet had a persuasive effect on people, so the four economists had to use every means to educate the undisciplined workers, persistently promoting the values of sacrifice, frugality, and self-control. Einaudi devoted himself assiduously to these themes: "If the newspapers preached abstinence and penitence to the newly rich, the peasants, and the workers, they would be performing a morally worthy and socially useful task."

Most experts today have not changed their rhetoric much. In a 1999 paper for the International Monetary Fund, Harvard economist Alberto Alesina targeted public sector employees, accusing them of creating a "culture of dependency," whereby residents in southern Italy "aspire to work in the public sector to take advantage of insurance benefits and the certainty of a permanent job." Privatization instead is necessary to prepare workers to "face the market."

In 2010, Alesina and his colleague Silvia Ardagna, chief European economist at Barclays, offered the same exact playbook as their fascist predecessors. They proposed supply-side reforms to deal with the European financial crisis, emphasizing the close link between fiscal austerity and industrial austerity as a way to discipline workers and increase investments. Cuts in social programs lead to reductions in public jobs and public wages, putting increased pressure on workers in the private sphere. In both cases, "the wage demanded by unions for private sector workers decreases, increasing profits, investments, and competitiveness." Later, Alesina suggested that for the good of all, policies of "wage moderation," "the cancellation of the Christmas related extra-payments," and raising the retirement age are desirable. Alesina's bitter comment foreshadowed vituperative policy debate in the runup to at least one election: "If the French think that they can keep retiring at 60, they're kidding themselves."

Deregulation of the labor market exposes workers to strong economic coercion and is among the primary causes of underpaid work in Italy. However, economists speak for the violent truth of our economy: worker insecurity is not a problem but an important competitive asset. People's well-being is certainly not a variable in the logic of capital. The economists' formula works: more precariousness means more disciplined workers and thus better conditions for capital accumulation.

Economic vulnerability and hardship fuel the rise of popular consent for xenophobic nationalist governments from Javier Milei in Argentina to Narendra Modi in India. These governments are the tangible expressions of the "success of austerity": its relentless application over decades has economically battered the majority, weakening people's ability to resist. Our material conditions leave little room for participating in class organizations or envisioning alternative futures. Instead, we fall prey to the narratives that stifle our collective ability to challenge the class hierarchies that oppress us. We blame those at the bottom of the social ladder. Immigrants who take our jobs and slackers living off benefits are the scapegoats of the moment.

The history of Nazi Germany is a case in point. Indeed, more than a decade of punishing austerity policies imposed by Germany's liberal governments—under pressure to meet the austerity mandates of the League of Nations—had the effect of crippling working-class movements in Germany, thereby opening the door for the far right to seize control and blame social problems on Jewish people and other minorities. If Mussolini gained support through his promise to eradicate economic democracy and dismantle organized labor, especially via austerity, Hitler's militarized and genocidal version of the austerity regime—repressing wages and labor rights to favor accumulation in the arms industry—was itself a direct consequence of the "success" of previous austerity.

Thus the full power of austerity emerges: it is functional to its own design. Austerity foments popular consensus for fascist-leaning governments that perpetuate further austerity policies. In a move reminiscent of Mussolini's policies a century ago—when he spearheaded one of the earliest large-scale privatization efforts in capitalist history—the Milei government, in just ten months, successfully privatized key sectors, including energy, water, sewage management, and railways. The Argentine state opened profitable pockets for private investors but condemned its people to higher utility bills, lower-quality service, and lower accountability. To look closer to home: In Pennsylvania, privatized water companies charged 84 percent more than public ones. In New Jersey, people on private systems pay 79 percent more.

When working-class people lose, our economic system wins. The austerity trinity supports capital, attracting wealthy investors through subsidies and state incentives, negligible taxes, low wages for workers, and minimal labor protections. Austerity ensures the best possible conditions for profits to skyrocket. In a burst of sincerity that is often lacking in mainstream economics, renowned investor Warren Buffett once said: "There's class warfare, all right, but it's my class, the rich class, that's making war, and we're winning."

The absence of dissenting voices makes this seem indisputable. But we can dispute the ways our economic predicaments are approached. Let's start with unemployment and inflation.

3.

THE CRUEL MATH OF UNEMPLOYMENT

Most economists do not even see unemployment beyond a number in a data set.

Dominant economic models have a blind faith in "equilibrium analysis" and essentially assume that the balancing forces of the market are efficient enough to guarantee full employment. If this does not happen, the responsibility isn't attributed to the market or the system in general. Rather, the triggering cause of unemployment is linked to so-called external factors, such as traumatic events (epidemics, wars), or to political interventions that stiffen the labor market (subsidies, minimum wages, etc.). As bizarre as this may sound, expert economists have argued that if workers are unemployed, it is simply because, due to excessive governmental benefits and regulation, they do not accept wages low enough to allow the labor supply to meet the demand. In other words, if things don't work out, the blame is always on the "bad" behavior of governments and workers. If workers were willing to sell their labor at the market price, they would have no difficulty finding buyers. The balance between supply and demand is always possible. The commodity known as labor power is not an exception but perfectly fits the rule.

These models are closely associated with the Chicago School of Economics, the most influential modern heir to the pure economics tradition. For decades, critical voices within economics have observed that today's mainstream approach, derived from the Chicago School and pure economics traditions, is utterly disconnected from reality. In the 1930s, John Maynard Keynes, writing from a position firmly within the scholarly establishment, described his colleagues as "Euclidean geometers in a non-Euclidean world." But despite its long-observed flaws, this distorted model has become the dominant organizing principle. Perhaps this shouldn't be surprising, since, as the celebrated critical economist James Kenneth Galbraith reminds us, distorted theories reveal how the economics discipline serves a political function:

> Modern economic belief can be understood only as the servant, in substantial measure, of the society which nurtures it. . . . Nor is the service less important for being rendered, in the main, in innocence and in the name of scientific truth. On the contrary, were it arranged and paid for it would cease to be of much effect. The wiles of the prostitute can be far more professional and superficially

compelling than those of her artless competition, but many more men succumb to the latter.

The role of neoclassical economists is not to explain society's deepest dynamics, but to support and buttress some convenient truth. It is certainly convenient for capitalism to claim that there is no escaping the market, and that the market functions efficiently in our best-of-all-possible worlds.

Let's try a different lens, that of critical economists, which allows us to grasp that the good conduct of workers matters little in ensuring full employment. In fact, it is the market that produces dangerous structural biases toward unemployment. In the words of Karl Marx, "It is capitalist accumulation itself that constantly produces . . . a relatively redundant working population, i.e. a population which is superfluous to capital's average requirements for its own valorization, and is therefore a surplus population."

Far from being the best of all possible worlds, the capitalist economy transforms the population into a reserve army. The "redundant working population" is the result of the very capital accumulation and economic growth we idolize.

This paradox, that the capitalist expansion of the economy systematically produces unemployment, runs directly counter to what many economists tell us. Growth and investment are supposed to eliminate unemployment, not create it. Yet the long-run dynamics of real competition belie this myth. To win the war of real competition, capital holders constantly invest in new technologies with the aim of increasing workers' productivity. Technological innovation and mechanization transform production. As accumulation progresses, more is spent on machines than on human labor. In other words, the economic system progresses through labor-saving technologies. Consider, for instance, the agricultural sector—the source of our food. In the middle of the nineteenth century, agriculture employed about 60 percent of US workers; now it employs only 10 percent of the workforce. This is largely due to technological advances such as tractors and mechanical seed drills that automate planting processes, allowing for fields to be cultivated by significantly fewer workers.

We can dispel the myth that under capitalism technological progress serves the primary function of fulfilling our human needs. Machines and technology are not at the service of the workers but turn into their nemeses. Workers are paid to produce technology that will render them redundant and replace them in many functions. Upon facing the masses "laid off by the machine," those lucky enough to keep their jobs will have to adjust to whatever pace the machines set.

To emerge victorious from competition, capitalists must make their employees work longer hours and with greater zeal to extract as much benefit as possible from the machinery. We therefore witness a further tendency of our economic system to create an "excess" or "redundant" population: if people could work fewer hours, the number of unemployed would be lower.

Contrary to what many economists believe, technology is not a neutral tool that can be abstracted from the economic context in which it arises. Within real competition, technology plays a vital role in the increase in profits. The latest innovations in artificial intelligence, such as ChatGPT, accelerate technological unemployment, threatening to render even the most specialized workers redundant, like analysts, engineers, and professors. So far, that has not yet happened, but jobs will be lost in any case. It's challenging to anticipate the social impact of these new technologies, and speculation is abundant. However, our critical lens provides at least one important insight. The consequences of AI are hard to predict not only because of the complexity of AI algorithms but because of the specific dynamics of our economy. Again, in our society, there is no economic plan formulated through collective decisions—whether democratic or authoritarian—but rather a myopic profusion of outcomes stemming from the individual decisions of large capital holders competing for survival and profit.

The hard truth is that the employment rate of the population within capitalism is at the mercy of capitalist decisions. Our livelihood depends on the profit expectations of a handful of corporations. If expectations don't look great, the employment rate won't look good. Obviously, if profit expectations are not high enough or are lower than production costs, particularly the costs of borrowed money, investors don't invest and workers don't get hired. Structural underemployment worsens during economic crises, when even the most optimistic investors hesitate to put money into production. Capital holders prefer to hoard or engage in financial speculation—for example, by buying their own shares of stock to artificially increase their value, a practice that's now widespread.

GDP growth is based on the exploitation of the majority—workers' unpaid labor—but it is paradoxically also workers who suffer the most from a declining GDP in a recessionary economy. In an economic crisis, workers risk losing their jobs. Fear of losing one's livelihood speaks to how unemployment is not only a consequence of capital accumulation but also a catalyst for it. Such fear safeguards our subordination to the capital order. Through our critical lens, we thus discover that a redundant population is a necessary element in the logic of capitalism.

A Frightening Truth

Far from being an exception determined by external factors, unemployment is the rule of the market. It gets worse: far from being a problem for our economic system, unemployment is crucial to its continued existence and development. The expanding ranks of the unemployed reserve army have driven the growth of capitalism from its beginnings.

When European governments colonized African countries and seized their immense natural resources, most intensively in the nineteenth century, they didn't immediately find workers. The countries' populations were entirely unfamiliar with the compulsion stemming from market dependence. Longstanding and harsh processes of dispossessing people from their means of subsistence—land, fishing opportunities, and other resources—laid the foundations for the success of corporations such as Shell Global that now invest in new oil fields (in the Niger Delta, for example) and that can easily recruit people willing to sell their labor power for low wages. This same surplus population is the main reason why today Amazon has no trouble opening new facilities worldwide. In fact, the corporation is courted by local governments through substantial tax breaks as a potential employer. In Italy, where youth unemployment reached 42.7 percent in 2014 and peaked at 55.9 percent in southern regions like Calabria and Sicily, policymakers pursued Amazon aggressively.

On the other hand, those who have pursued and won employment are profoundly dissatisfied with their jobs. According to the 2023 Censis-Eudaimon report on corporate welfare, 46.7 percent of workers in Italy are unhappy and would like to leave their current occupation, with higher numbers among youths. One of the reasons for this discontent is that 65 percent report a lack of career opportunities. According to Gallup's *Global Workplace* report, employee engagement is low on all five continents. Almost two-thirds of workers are not fulfilled by what they do and adopt a utilitarian view of work— the idea that it "only serves to provide the money I need." For many, even this goal remains elusive, as a lack of gratification and recognition is accompanied by poor pay, meaning it's difficult to make ends meet. Despite the humiliation and frustration, more than half of those employed are not inclined to leave their jobs. Why? A lack of alternatives. As the sociology professor Francesca Coin wrote about the reality of the Italian economy, "This is hardly a reassuring picture, indicating a work normality marked by insecurity and dissatisfaction, in which the desire for change is solely discouraged by the fear of not finding another job."

In Italy, as in many other countries, unemployment plays a primary role in creating a sense of material and psychological powerlessness that hinders collective challenges to the capitalist pillar of wage labor. Fear of losing employment is what holds our system together, yet this is underplayed by many economists, even a great like Keynes. The British scholar highlighted that the market economy tends to generate underemployment, but he never questioned his colleagues' dismissal of exploitation from their models. Indeed, he assumed that labor and capital were both equal inputs of the production process, a parable of cooperation between capital and labor in the production of goods and services. In this apolitical framework, unemployment is seen as a "technical" problem, solvable through good public policies aimed at full employment.

In 1943, the Polish economist Michał Kalecki, one of the most important and innovative theorists of the past century, reflected that within capitalism, eliminating unemployment might be a technical possibility, but it certainly is not a political one. He argued, "Under a regime of permanent full employment, the 'sack' would cease to play its role as a disciplinary measure . . . [creating] political tension" in a short article titled "Political Aspects of Full Employment," which warned against Keynesian technocratic optimism.

Hypothetically, with full employment, workers could gain enough political freedom to challenge the very foundation of capitalism—the relationship of exploitation. Imagine Walmart workers saying to their managers, "If you don't pay us better, we're going to stop working." If no unemployed person were available to take that job, Walmart would have to raise wages. At that point, the workers might push further, questioning the very idea of wage labor and demanding a share in the company's profits and decision-making. This has happened before, after all. The demands of Walmart workers could extend to other sectors, putting the very stability of our economic system at risk. By contrast, a certain level of unemployment ensures our passive resignation to the system while maintaining the "right" balance of power between capital and labor. The reserve army is the pivot on which the law of supply and demand for labor rests: it confines the scope of this law within the unbreachable and highly convenient limits of capital exploitation and dominance.

The struggle for unionization of Amazon workers in Bessemer, Alabama, peaked in the summer of 2022. The primary reason most employees were afraid to vote in favor of a union fighting for more humane working hours and conditions was the intimidating threat of being replaced. Employers speak a universal language: "Don't like the working conditions? Fine, we'll relocate to another part of the country where people can't wait to be hired and work for us."

With the threat of unemployment, workers are pitted against one another and are willing to accept higher levels of exploitation, allowing companies to sell their products at lower prices through wage suppression and maintain their competitive advantage. Marx captured this dynamic: "The over-work of the employed part of the working class swells the ranks of its reserve, while, conversely, the greater pressure that the reserve by its competition exerts on the employed workers forces them to submit to over-work and subjects them to the dictates of capital."

Worldwide, political parties and governments benefit from these internal antagonisms within the working class. Especially in times of high social discontent, they fan the flames of hatred among the weak, directing it against those even weaker. Restrictive immigration laws—introduced not coincidentally after the end of colonialism and slavery—are framed as protections for working-class citizens but actually fabricate the political conditions for further economic confiscation that benefits capital accumulation—namely, a body of workers exceptionally vulnerable to the demands of capital. State border policies swell the ranks of the reserve army with those who, lacking basic legal rights, are subject to what the American philosopher Nancy Fraser calls "expropriability": "the condition of being defenseless, and liable to violation, that constitutes the core of racial oppression."

This reliance on a stratum of unfree and subjugated people, racially marked as inherently violable, is crucial to lowering production costs. Consider Italy's tomato-sauce export business, which peaked at 4.4 billion euros ($4.62 billion) in sales in 2022, making Italy the third largest exporter after the United States and China. The fancy cans you find in supermarkets worldwide rely heavily on migrant workers who labor more than twelve hours a day, earn 3 euros ($3.40) for 300 kilos (660 pounds) of tomatoes, and often die from heat exhaustion. They endure inhumane working conditions in which fires break out in their lodgings and burn people alive every summer. Similarly, the vast infrastructure for the 2022 FIFA World Cup in Qatar was built through the sweat of thousands of Nepalese migrant workers, who toiled in slave-like conditions and suffered wage theft. The prosperous US meatpacking industry would potentially collapse without undocumented workers, who earn less than the legal minimum wage and suffer from wage theft and injuries. On average there are two amputations a week across US meat plants.

Unemployment fosters a sense of insecurity and destroys solidarity among workers, who often divide into racial or ethnic factions, and then fail to protect the most vulnerable.

If the political conditions maintaining the reserve army disappear, capitalism falls into deep crisis. In the United States, in the early 2020s, the unemployment rate hit historic lows, dropping to 3.4 percent in January 2023. Let's take a closer look at this figure. A 3.4 percent unemployment rate still represents approximately 5.7 million people out of work. Moreover, this figure includes only people actively seeking employment and excludes those who have become discouraged and stopped looking. Among the latter are inevitably a large proportion of mothers and racial minorities. The Bureau of Labor Statistics considers anyone "who has done any paid work during the survey reference week" as employed, which means even the most insecurely employed workers are counted. All of this indicates that the actual number of individuals lacking stable employment is higher—maybe double.

The fact that even a 4 percent unemployment rate is considered "alarming" for the capital order discloses the bleak character of our economy. Experts complain that today's labor market is "tight to an unhealthy level" with too few available workers to fill the job openings, as Federal Reserve Chair Jerome Powell has said. In the United States between 2021 and 2023, the law of supply and demand was, for once, favoring the workers: despite monetary tightening, there were still four job openings for every job seeker, and nominal wages increased beyond what employers were willing to bear. Of course, real wages remained stagnant, but employers were worried, and not only about rising costs of labor.

When technocrats use terms like "healthy" and "appropriate" to describe the economy, they focus on capital accumulation rather than the needs of people and their living conditions. A labor market that is even slightly favorable to employees encourages workers to push to reduce the rate of exploitation. This happened in the United States during the post-pandemic recovery: the increased bargaining power of workers led to stronger organizations, new unionizations, and a surge in strikes that ultimately increased wages.

The United Auto Workers (UAW) strike exemplifies the changing dynamics in labor movements. It began on September 15, 2023, and lasted almost seven weeks. It was astonishing not only for the number of participants (about 150,000 from the UAW) but also for the fact that workers from the "Big Three" of the automotive sector—General Motors, Ford, and Stellantis (Fiat Chrysler)—united in the same battle. While shareholders' wealth had risen and CEOs' salaries had increased by 40 percent in the four years prior to the strike, employee wages had grown by only 6 percent, effectively resulting in a loss of purchasing power because of inflation. These companies have accumulated around $250 billion in profits over the past decade, bolstered by government subsidies and austerity imposed on workers. With new public subsidies for the green transition to electric vehicles, profit expectations for the three corporations soared, but workers demanded a change of direction. And they won their demands: a new thirty-two-hour workweek contract, the restoration of cost-of-living adjustments, workplace safety protections, and a 40 percent pay increase over four years.

The UAW strike followed a surge of strikes in various industries, reflecting growing discontent across a wide spectrum of workers. In logistics, workers at UPS and Amazon were vocal in their demands, asking for better pay, improved safety, and job security. Hospitality workers at hotels and Starbucks, alongside railroad employees, teachers, and nurses, joined the wave with strikes of their own. In 2022, the number of strikes rose by 52 percent from the previous year, while participation increased by 60 percent. For instance, Hollywood writers went on strike for 146 days and significantly challenged corporate practices. Their success included higher wages, increased pension funding, and safeguards against replacement by artificial intelligence.

Workers were unafraid to use the most explicit forms of class conflict to challenge an economy that works only for a few, and is leading to a climate catastrophe. Workers asserted a fundamental truth: "We are the ones who produce value."

The establishment's preoccupations ring strikingly familiar to the ones in the 1920s. CNN alluded to the unreasonableness of the UAW's demands: "The union went on strike despite offers from the companies to raise hourly wages as much as 20% over the life of the contracts." In an article titled "The UAW Won Big in the Auto Strike—but What Does It Mean for the Rest of Us?," NPR warned that "rising wages and any increase in auto prices would put upward pressure on inflation", while a *New York Times* headline spread fear: "U.A.W. Strike Gains Could Reverberate Far Beyond Autos."

This recent history suggests that the conditions for maintaining smooth capital accumulation are never guaranteed.

Inflation

These thoughts allow us to tackle the elephant in capitalism's living room. Inflation, meaning the general increase in prices, is the people's foe. Anything we buy, from milk to gas, costs more, and the first to bear the consequences are working families who have smaller cash reserves.

Neoclassical economists are well aware of the close link between the labor market and the monetary sphere. This connection is described by the Phillips curve, a model that continues to serve as an indispensable reference point for technocrats shaping monetary policies. In 1957, the economist William Phillips empirically observed a negative correlation between the unemployment rate and nominal wages: the higher the number of unemployed, the lower wages would be. Over time, the curve that bears his name has evolved to also capture a negative correlation between the number of unemployed and price stability. In other words, the higher the rate of unemployment, the less prices will increase, and therefore inflation will be lower.

College students learn about the Phillips curve, studying it as if it were merely a mathematical equation to memorize in order to pass an exam. However, its ugly political meaning cannot be reduced to a simple arithmetic exercise. The Phillips curve lays bare the inherent violence and even irrationality of a society that decides to organize production according to the logic of private profit.

When there are fewer unemployed workers, employed workers gain bargaining power and can demand higher wages. Indeed, in a tight labor market, companies are forced to compete against one another for workers by offering better wages and benefits. If wages rise, the system risks getting jammed, since producers will either stop producing or pass on the higher labor costs to consumers (who are the workers themselves) by raising prices. The result is inflation. Companies decide to raise prices to offset the increase in costs so that profits are unaffected.

The Phillips curve packages the unpalatable trade-off between profits and unemployment into the more palatable one between inflation and unemployment. This seemingly innocuous choice of variables achieves important wins for the system. By hiding what is really at stake—the protection of profits—it focuses our attention on inflation. We are all led to believe that economists are primarily concerned with combating inflation, a phenomenon that especially hurts those with less purchasing power. So we easily overlook the violent reality of our economy: without unemployment there is no smooth investment.

This is nowhere more evident than in the concept of the so-called natural rate of unemployment, or non-accelerating inflation rate of unemployment (NAIRU). It evolved from the Phillips curve and argues that the economy has a natural rate of unemployment and that any attempt to push unemployment below this level will result in accelerating inflation. The NAIRU transforms a pain that is specific to capitalism into one that is supposedly unavoidable. It tells us that unemployment is not a political choice stemming from the economic system we have constructed but a fact of human affairs, stemming from the laws of nature themselves.

Economic models and the policies that follow are built in such a way that it's always the workers who have to make sacrifices. For there to be monetary stability, there must be a significant number of people without jobs. If hiring were to exceed what many mainstream economists define as the "natural" threshold tolerable by the system, the lives of the employed people wouldn't become easier, because it could trigger an inflationary cycle that would erode wages.

Indeed, economists and anyone concerned about the stability of capitalism will hope that workers do not organize to obtain wage hikes (in excess of increases in labor productivity), to avoid triggering the infamous wage-price spiral that could cripple our system. Out-of-control prices risk eroding consent toward the economic order, leading to strikes and clashes, and even the questioning of the very pillars of capitalism. Inflationary crises are among the strongest threats to the integrity of the capital order. These are the moments when people recognize how a society that has decided to produce and distribute goods through the price mechanism of the market is neither efficient nor just; the rationing criteria is all about who has the money. It's how we accept a situation in which a minority can hoard goods while the rest can barely eat.

Solutions to inflation that don't presuppose workers' sacrifices exist, to be sure. Think about the price caps and taxes on corporations that have been enacted, especially in moments of political emergency, for example, during the two world wars. However, given that they operate counter to the logic of capital accumulation, they require a political battle that ultimately implies questioning the foundations of our economic system. If ever introduced, they may initiate the road toward a different economic organization.

Contrary to how it is presented in economics textbooks, the wage-price spiral is not automatic, it is not deterministic, it is not a fact of the universe; rather, it is the result of specific political decisions made by those who hold capital and who do not want to (or cannot) bear the burden of increasing labor costs. As critical economist Richard D. Wolff emphasizes, inflation embodies the quintessentially antidemocratic nature of our economic organization. Indeed, there is nothing transcendent about price setting: corporations are the ones that set prices. Neoclassical economics hides this reality with its abstraction about perfectly competitive markets. In these economists' wage-price narrative, the silent blame for inflation falls on workers, seen as responsible for the imbalance that jeopardizes society as we know it, rather than on corporations.

The classism of the economic models that guide public debate and economic policy is hidden in plain sight. It is assumed that inflation is due to exceedingly low unemployment rates, resulting in higher wages and increased household consumption. Lawrence H. Summers, former president of Harvard University, an adviser to President Barack Obama, and still one of the most influential public voices asserted: "Rising demand, with capacity and labor constraints, are fully sufficient to account for what we observe in meatpacking [higher prices]." Workers are scolded for consuming too much and working too little. This interpretation precludes the circulation of more critical explanations that speak of a "profit epidemic." According to these empirical studies, far from being the fault of labor costs and unemployment rates, the increase in prices is primarily attributable to the political decisions of the ruling class, resulting in profit margins that are at an all-time high both in Europe and the United States.

But a critical approach urges us to avoid simplifications. Economist Robert Reich stresses that inflation is profit-led rather than wage-driven, but he remains deeply entrenched in the model that idealizes the market and is favored by Summers and so many others. According to Reich, the cause of the problem lies in monopolies that can manipulate prices, which compromise the efficiency of the system by hindering free competition. But our critical lens shows that price manipulation does not get at the heart of the problem. It is precisely the dynamics of the market that lead to the centralization of capital typical of monopolies, which then have unchecked power to hike prices. The problem of inflation cannot be solved with more free market competition.

How does a society in which the majority is exploited by a small minority manage to stay afloat? If there's nothing natural about it, how is the social relationship that underpins our economic growth preserved? We have analyzed how the trends of real competition and capitalist accumulation generate structural unemployment and how this phenomenon is not a flaw in the system but represents its lifeblood. The reserve army keeps us docile because we are precarious and replaceable. Even if we have terrible job hours, receive meager paychecks, don't see our children, and spend more time working than doing anything else, what do we have to complain about? We should be grateful we have a job. To fully grasp the deeply political nature of our economy, it is crucial to stress how these power imbalances are actively consolidated through governmental economic decisions, especially with austerity. The state, in fact, never loses its resolute role as a protector of the market. Unemployment must be "created" to keep our system alive—a system that prioritizes the health of capital, not people.

Summers has no doubt that increasing unemployment rates for the well-being of the US economy is a "necessity." "Fighting inflation will require a decrease in vacancies and an increase in unemployment. There is no magic tool," he wrote in a July 2022 report coauthored with his colleagues Olivier Blanchard and Alex Domash.

In July 2024, high interest rates achieved their primary goal of increasing the unemployment rate by a percentage point in one year. An additional 1.3 million Americans were without work—not counting the more than half a million workers who were forced to accept part-time, precarious positions because of a lack of full-time opportunities. While many critical economists dispute that high interest rates actually help tame inflation—especially if it is a profit-driven one—what is indisputable is that through monetary austerity, Fed officials create the conditions for wage compression: people are no longer able to hold off from accepting crummy jobs with lousy pay. And this is what ultimately matters.

As my mentor Professor Duncan Foley put it, monetary and fiscal policies targeting inflation should really be described as "rate-of-exploitation targeting." This becomes all the more apparent when we look beyond national policies to the hard-fought battles of the ruling elites to maintain a stable globalized capitalist economy, where capital is free to move unencumbered in search of lower labor costs.

4.

THE WEST OVER THE REST

Mussolini succeeded in presenting his country to the capitalist world as an economically respectable power. Thanks to austerity, by 1925 the conditions for capital accumulation had been secured: strikes and unions were outlawed, profit rates climbed, and international capital flowed in.

The more recent Italian governments of Mario Draghi and Giorgia Meloni are appreciated by international markets precisely because they fit the good books of international creditors and investors. The spread between German bonds and those of other European countries decreases, credit ratings improve, and everyone applauds. However, the "forced choice" of austerity that leads to more positive credit ratings certainly does not allow for a sigh of relief: on the contrary, it tightens the coercive grip of real competition and forges the path toward more austerity policies with greater vigor year after year, to the point that now strategic national sectors are sold to international asset managers, from telecommunications to agriculture.

This capital trap, which Italy experiences firsthand as a periphery of Europe, is even more ferocious in the global periphery, where the austerity motto "Consume less, produce more," perpetuated since colonial times, leads to devastating results.

Development economists whose research appears in the most prestigious academic journals—from the *American Economic Review* to the *Review of Development Economics*—receive the bulk of their funding from wealthy foundations to run randomized control trials that treat the people of the Global South like experimental rats. Such research studies often reduce countrywide dynamics to the decision-making of individuals, investigating how people's choices may not be rational due to a failure to manage resources optimally. The narrow focus on individuals, in particular how poor people can make better decisions for themselves, takes for granted the macroeconomic context that produces poverty.

Other studies evaluate the stages of economic growth of various countries to assess how far they are from supposedly catching up to their developed counterparts. This exercise in pure ideology dates back to the Massachusetts Institute of Technology professor Walt Rostow, who served as an adviser to the Kennedy and Johnson administrations and played a key role in shaping US foreign policy in Southeast Asia during the Cold War. As a prominent promoter of the capitalist economic system, Rostow wrote an influential essay called "The Stages of Economic Growth: A Non-Communist Manifesto" to feed the illusion that the US's linear path to development could be transplanted as a one-size-fits-all template for any nation interested in pursuing economic growth. The key to success was, of course, more capitalism, more global markets.

These ideas that keep benefiting those elites who spread them have the lure of optimism. It is enough to conform and things will get better. As economists James Kenneth Galbraith and Jing Chen eloquently put it: "Since poor countries are called developing countries, their conditions are expected to improve over time. Overall, global conditions will improve indefinitely, with only occasional temporary setbacks. When improvements don't occur, it must be due to institutional deficiencies that distort market functions, such as corruption or 'crony capitalism.'" Yet the data speaks clearly: Global North countries control 69 percent of global wealth, and 77 percent of billionaire wealth, and are home to 68 percent of billionaires, despite making up just 21 percent of the global population. On the other hand, there are 1.8 billion people, representing almost a quarter of the world's population, who live on less than $3.65 a day.

Catching up is a mirage under the current rules of the game, as it is structurally incompatible with the logic and function of the capitalist economy. Far from accepting that African countries are poor because they have not yet implemented enough market reforms, we can see that it is the opening to global capitalism that reinforces their subordination.

As critical scholars Andre Gunder Frank and Samir Amin argue, Western development does not emerge independently from the rest of the world. On the contrary, development results from the active creation of *underdevelopment*. Simply, there would be no wealth in the US and Europe without the construction of poverty in the rest of the world.

Indeed, those who follow the lure of capital accumulation are on the hunt for the best game. The countries that are richest in terms of natural resources—from oil to minerals to food—are the first to fall prey. Ghana, for example, which is currently experiencing one of its worst economic crises in a generation, and where poverty, hunger, and child malnutrition are widespread, is rich in gold, cocoa, diamonds, and manganese. Foreign multinational corporations engage in raw material extraction, leaving very little for the Ghanaians.

While primary resources are siphoned out of countries like Ghana, companies in the Global North that have the industrial capacity to build more and cheaper commodities can successfully sell them to the African markets. The global division of labor has made Rostow's promised path of development for much of the globe impossible. In the early stages of capitalism, colonial powers actively suppressed the development of domestic industries in their colonies, but in the last century the open-border system for goods and capital has undermined local manufacturing, achieving the same goal of economic dominance.

As economist Ha-Joon Chang has shown, in past centuries developed countries built their industrial capacity through forms of protectionism: shutting their doors to international competition and lavishly subsidizing their national producers to invest in capital-intensive production. Ironically, the decision-making elite largely based in the US and in Europe now prevent countries of the Global South from doing the same: they impose the "free" trade and the "free" markets. Without the ability to compete with international producers, Ghana has no option but to import the majority of technology and manufactured goods, from refrigerators to cars.

Critical economists have captured the dynamics described above with the concept of dependency. Dependency theory explains how the movement of primary resources from the periphery to the center and the movement of final goods from the center to the periphery locks nations on the periphery in a vicious cycle. These poorer nations are unable to develop their productive base, which increases their trade deficit and keeps them dependent on the goods market and labor market of the center. The economic structure of the periphery morphs into whatever the center demands. The result is underdevelopment.

The trap is structural to Ghana and all other such countries: when the balance of trade worsens, this means that imports exceed exports. With more money flowing out than is coming in, countries must borrow to continue financing their imports. Thus foreign debt skyrockets. In this way, another relation of dependency is created, that of foreign loans, which lead to even more wealth flowing out of the country as interest on debt mounts.

Technocratic institutions such as the International Monetary Fund and the World Bank fortify a relationship of dependency. In June 2024, Ghana took out its eighteenth IMF loan since independence, all of which were conditional on strict austerity. Between 1997 and 2003, some thirty-seven countries were forced to renegotiate their debts and undergo austerity restructuring. The IMF required them to sell their national assets to private companies; relax restrictions on foreign capital investment, making it easier for foreign companies to take control of key industries; and deregulate their financial markets.

Argentina is one of the most infamous examples of IMF intervention. During the 1980s and 1990s, the IMF provided Argentina with multiple loans to "rescue" the country from debt. These loans came with harsh austerity conditions, leading to deep cuts to social spending, such as pensions and education, while foreign and national investors were lured by attractive deals on newly privatized sectors, lower taxes, and weakened worker protections. In 1998, when the economy entered a deep depression, a $22 billion IMF loan package resulted in more of the same social suffering but not much of the promised economic stability. By 2001 Argentina's economy had collapsed, causing the largest sovereign debt default in history at that time.

Western governments boast about aid to so-called developing countries, but humanitarian aid is a facade. Many empirical studies confirm that, at the level of the most simpleminded accounting, more money flows out of Africa than goes in. The most impoverished continent is a "net creditor" to the rest of the world. In 2015, African countries received $162 billion, mainly in loans, aid, and personal remittances. But in the same year, $203 billion was taken from the continent, either directly through capital flight, when multinationals repatriate profits to their home countries, or indirectly through the payment of interests on loans. A report from the Political Economy Research Institute at the University of Massachusetts at Amherst shows that over the past five decades, thirty sub-Saharan African countries have lost more than $2 trillion to capital flight, which is almost the annual gross domestic product of sub-Saharan Africa. This hemorrhage has accelerated since the turn of the century, averaging $65 billion a year, a sum that far exceeds annual inflows of official development aid. The more the peripheral states are pushed to privatize, the more these resource-rich countries transform their wealth into dividends for international private shareholders. Oxfam reports that in 2024 the superrich in the Global North extracted $30 million an hour from the Global South.

Countries in the Global South are stuck in a perennial ditch. They are told that foreign capital and investment are the way out of poverty, but these in fact dig the ditch deeper. Foreign capital has no incentive to risk its funds with long-term developmental projects, preferring investment in sectors like natural resource extraction and construction, where surplus value is created from cheap labor. Pressure to attract foreign capital, or at least prevent capital flight, induces monetary authorities in peripheral countries to keep their interest rates high in order to convince investors that their currency will not collapse. In an effort to remain integrated into the global capital system, these countries lose all autonomy in economic policymaking. In this way, austerity policies are not merely imposed by external bodies like the IMF; rather, they are embedded in the very structure of financial markets and the process of capital accumulation.

Even when exports are high and the country ticks the boxes of "good fundamentals," the markets don't stop their disciplinary scrutiny. The reelection of a leader like Luiz Inácio Lula da Silva in Brazil in 2023—or any leader perceived as overly supportive of social redistribution—is punished with financial speculation against the country's currency: a means to pressure these governments to do more austerity than their predecessors have done. It is no surprise that Lula nominated a "prudent" chief of the central bank and promised to achieve a zero-deficit goal in 2025.

Adding insult to injury, the losers of the global capital relations game are also those who are facing the worst effects of the unfolding climate catastrophe. The floods in Brazil's Rio Grande do Sul in 2024 left 1,000 people either killed or injured and 150,000 homeless. That same year, southern Africa experienced its worst drought in a century, leaving more than 21 million children deeply malnourished as crops failed. These climate disasters are very bad news for people who are threatened by famine and destruction, but as philosopher Kohei Saito points out, the constant extraction that underpins our capitalist economy is largely made invisible to citizens in the Global North. And international capitalists have even found a silver lining. The climate mitigation efforts of the African and Latin American governments are all novel market opportunities for foreign businesses to take advantage of.

Israel over Palestine

Israel doesn't obviously represent the West, but it has set up Palestinian economic dependence in a way that is analogous to what the West has established over the rest of the world.

A Palestinian worker writes of his daily life:

At 7:30 a.m. you wake up, you want to take a shower, but you have to buy water from Mekorot, Israel's water company that has taken control of 80 percent of the West Bank's water resources. At 8:30 a.m., get in the car to go to work.... In the West Bank, the Israeli army has a network of 97 fixed checkpoints and hundreds of "flying" checkpoints, which appear and disappear without warning. Long queues, document checks, often closures—collective or to individuals—without explanation. Every Palestinian worker must leave home well in advance. On the lunch break, to buy a sandwich or go shopping, only the Israeli shekel is used, as we have never had a Palestinian currency. Maybe you have to buy gasoline, only from Israeli operators, who have total control of energy resources.

Over the last one hundred years, the economic structure of Palestine has been transformed to serve Israel's economy. Proof of this is Israel's GDP per person: twice that of Palestine's in 1967, it dwarfed Palestine's by over 25 times and Gaza's by 150 by 2022.

Over time, as economist Ibrahim Shikaki has uncovered, the Palestinian economy has lost both its independent manufacturing and agricultural bases. The extraction of value is therefore all in favor of Israel, which benefits on the one hand from receiving raw materials, such as land, water, minerals, and labor, and on the other hand from a market to sell its goods. Conversely, the Palestinian territories must import expensive finished goods, developing a trade deficit that increases their economic vulnerability. In the past fifty years, more than 75 percent of Palestine's imports and exports have been traded with Israel. Nearly half of all goods imported from Israel were previously produced in Palestine, including clothing, footwear, soft drinks, furniture, pharmaceuticals, and even construction supplies.

To study how political decisions led to Palestinian economic dependence, we need to consider the years of the British Mandate, 1922 to 1948. Britain played a crucial role in leading the Palestinian economy in a capitalist direction in collaboration with Zionist organizations such as the Palestine Jewish Colonization Association, the Jewish National Fund, and the Palestine Land Development Company. Indeed, the British Empire enabled these organizations to purchase and privatize vast amounts of common land, which was then registered as "land only for Jews," no longer salable to non-Jews. Palestinians were thus detached from the land that formed the basis of their subsistence economy and underwent the key social transition to market dependence and wage labor.

Moreover, the British Empire demanded agricultural taxes in money rather than, as had previously been the case, in agricultural goods that peasants could produce themselves. This drove Palestinian peasants into debt, since they were forced to borrow at high interest rates, reinforcing their condition of market dependence. Meanwhile, Britain encouraged investment in Jewish industries and granted concessions on natural resources to Jewish companies, including key resource companies such as the Atlit Salt Company (1922), the Palestine Electric Company (1923), and the Palestine Potash Company (1929).

The British Mandate's unequal tariff policies strengthened the conditions of Palestinian dependence. The British abolished both export tariffs on Jewish-produced goods and import tariffs on the raw materials they required. At the same time, Britain imposed high import tariffs on foreign goods, such as cement and chemicals, that could compete with Jewish industries. The opposite treatment was given to Arab-produced goods. No import tariffs were placed on foreign goods that could compete with Arab-dominated industries like soap, olive oil, and agricultural products. Indeed, Britain's enforcement of an open border policy on agriculture, previously tested in India, punished Palestinian farmers, who had to struggle to compete with imported food products, which increased their debt and eventually forced many to sell their land to large landowners.

After twenty-five years under the British Mandate, the Jewish economy had significantly outpaced its Arab counterpart. The Jewish share of national production had risen to 53 percent and the share of manufacturing production to 89 percent. Jewish capital investments accounted for 88 percent of the region's total investments. These were the conditions at the time of the 1947 United Nations partition plan, after which the state of Israel was created and Palestinians experienced the first of their catastrophes. During the Nakba, which lasted seven months, more than 530 villages were destroyed, over fifteen thousand civilians were killed, and 80 percent of the Palestinian population became refugees. Palestine was reduced to less than a quarter of the territory of Mandate Palestine, now only including the West Bank, Gaza Strip, and East Jerusalem.

The key moment in the construction of Palestine's political-economic subjugation, however, was the Israeli occupation of the West Bank, Gaza, and East Jerusalem in 1967. Israel enforced its currency as the official one for the Palestinian territories, replacing previously used regional currencies, and took full control of the fiscal budget in the West Bank and Gaza, overseeing taxation and collection. Palestinians were forced to pay income taxes that were 3 to 10 percent higher than Israelis in the same income bracket.

Between 1967 and 1971, the Israeli military issued over two hundred orders regulating Palestinian economic life. Among them, the closure of all thirty bank branches operating in the West Bank and Gaza except for two, which were placed under Israeli supervision; the prohibition of investment from Israel—or from abroad—in the Palestinian economy; the ban on importing new machines (Palestinian firms could purchase only secondhand machines); and the imposition of a complex web of administrative procedures and restrictions, still in place today, that make it virtually impossible for Palestinians to start a business. Between 2016 and 2018, Israeli military authorities approved only 3 percent of building permits in the largest part of the West Bank under its direct control, known as Area C.

An important milestone in the codification of economic dependence was the signing of the 1994 Paris Protocol—part of the Oslo Accords—which remains the formal economic framework governing relations between Israel and the Palestinian Authority. The Palestinian Authority, established that same year, became the official governing body of the Palestinian territories, albeit with limited sovereignty. The protocol was intended as a transitional arrangement, with the expectation that a final peace agreement would pave the way for a fully sovereign Palestinian state. Such an agreement has yet to be achieved.

On paper, the Palestinian Authority gained several key economic responsibilities, including the ability to collect income taxes within the West Bank and Gaza Strip and, through the newly established Palestinian Monetary Authority, the capacity to exercise monetary control—but without the authority to issue currency.

However, the Paris Protocol's stated goal of allowing the Palestinian Authority to exercise "its right of economic decision-making in accordance with its own development plan and priorities" was undermined by the imbalance of economic and political power between Israel and the Palestinian territories. The one-sided operation of the newly formed customs union between Israel and the Palestinian territories is a case in point, exemplifying a form of colonial supremacy. Israel controls the borders: all goods imported or exported by Palestinians must pass through Israeli customs, which can block, seize, or impose restrictions on goods. These obstacles create high transportations costs, forcing private importers to increase their prices and resulting in permanent inflation for the Palestinian people.

Israel has the power to unilaterally establish and change the taxes imposed on goods imported into Palestine. It collects import taxes and is supposed to transfer these clearance funds to the Palestinian Authority on a monthly basis. But for years Israel has been withholding them in part or in their entirety. This is no trifling sum of money: in 2022, Israel withheld $3.1 billion, which was 65 percent of the Palestinian government's total annual revenue. Israel has withheld these funds to punish Palestinian acts of resistance, especially the attempt to seek international support for national autonomy. When the Palestinians sought UN and UNESCO membership in 2011, Israel withheld $100 million. Later, in response to Palestine's acceptance as a nonmember state of the UN in 2012, clearance funds were withheld for three months. In the winter of 2015, Israel froze another $450 million after Palestine took steps to join the International Criminal Court.

Israel's power to turn off the money faucet is ultimately the power to impose austerity on the Palestinian people. The Palestinian Authority cannot provide essential public services and has been forced to cut stipends for public employees, including teachers and health care workers who make up almost a quarter of the Palestinian labor force. From October 2023 to January 2025, Israel withheld over $1 billion in funds, money that should have gone to pay for the administrative expenses of Gaza. As a result, Palestinian public employees saw their salaries reduced by up to 50 percent. Austerity inevitably leads to greater financial dependency: the Palestinian government has no choice but to borrow heavily from private Israeli banks, enhancing Israel's profits and diverting more public funds down the road to interest payments.

The dependency-austerity trap is exacerbated by the extraction of resources from the Palestinian population, such as electricity and water. In a telling example, the sum Israel agreed to release from the clearance funds in January 2025 (technically owed to the Palestinian government as their tax revenue) never reached the Palestinian Authority and instead went directly to an Israeli state-run electricity company in payment for past debts.

Israeli appropriation of water, the most vital resource for the operation of an economy, and of human life for that matter, is the most dramatic example of Palestinian economic dependence. Before the Israeli occupation of 1967, water was a common resource accessible to all. But after the occupation, the Israeli military placed all water resources in Palestinian territories under its control, prohibiting Palestinians from constructing new water installations or maintaining existing installations without a military permit. These orders are still in place.

According to a 2021 report from the United Nations, colonial appropriation has led to outright destruction. In 2020, 84 of the 849 structures destroyed in the West Bank by Israel were water and sanitation structures, and Israeli authorities have repeatedly blocked Palestinian projects relating to the development and maintenance of water infrastructure. Palestinians in the West Bank are thus forced to purchase 80 percent of their annual water supply from Mekorot, Israel's state-owned national water company. Mekorot assumed ownership of all West Bank water supply systems in 1982 and systematically provides privileged water access to the Israeli settlements in the West Bank. As the report explains: "Mekorot prioritizes Israeli settlements to ensure their permanent water supply, in particular during summer droughts. Palestinian communities connected to the Mekorot network often suffer lengthy water outages, while neighbouring settlements are largely spared any significant water reduction."

Even before the genocide in Gaza and the annihilation of almost all of the territory's infrastructure, the situation there was much worse. According to the World Bank, the water supply in Gaza has been at "crisis levels" since 2005. UNICEF reported that in 2020 only 10 percent of the population in Gaza had direct access to clean and safe drinking water. Palestinians in Gaza were prevented from drilling wells and importing materials such as cement and iron needed to repair water infrastructure. At the same time, the chronic electricity deficit also heavily impaired functional water management. These past years have shown that economic dependency can easily be transformed into a genocidal instrument. After October 2023, Israel cut off electricity to Gaza, making the desalination of water dependent on fuel, which was also subjected to repeated blockades of one hundred days or longer. This catastrophic man-made drought has meant that thousands of children have died of thirst and suffered from diarrhea, scabies, and polio.

The transformation of the Palestinian labor force is another element that benefits Israel. Over the years, the Palestinian economy has been rendered structurally incapable of employing its own workers, who must turn to whatever employment Israel decides fit to offer. Self-sufficient agricultural communities have seen their livelihoods disappear. Land confiscations, which peaked between the mid-1970s and mid-1980s, and restrictions on trade, investment, and water access caused the collapse of the Palestinian agricultural sector. In 1967, nearly 40 percent of the total labor force worked in agriculture, a number that dropped to less than 20 percent by 1993 and to 3 percent in 2017.

The result has been a dramatic class shift: Palestinians who were once self-employed in agriculture became wage workers in the Israeli economy. In 1967 half of economically active Palestinians were self-employed, with virtually no one from the Palestinian territories working in Israel. However, twenty years later the number of self-employed had decreased by half, and 40 percent of Palestinian workers were crossing the borders to sell their labor power to Israeli employers. This shift has paradoxically exacerbated the fragility of the Palestinian economy. When the Israeli military closes checkpoints, the Palestinian unemployment rate almost automatically surges. Moreover, when Israel allows Palestinians to work within its borders, Palestinians use increased wages to buy Israeli commodities. Given the lack of local manufacturing, Palestinians often have no choice but to buy these Israeli goods. Thus the greater purchasing power of Palestinian workers directly translates into greater trade deficits and greater profits for Israeli exporters. The grip of dependence really couldn't be stronger.

Palestinian labor boosts the profits of Israeli capitalists in multiple ways. Ibrahim Shikaki has shown how the Palestinian reserve army helps pacify the conflict between capital and labor in Israel by taking away bargaining power from Israeli workers. The construction of a pool of cheap Palestinian labor keeps the wages of Israeli workers in check. Moreover, Israeli employers pay Palestinians more than they could earn in the domestic economy, yet less than their Israeli counterparts, ensuring higher profits for Israeli businesses. As one owner put it in the newspaper *Davar*: "It is almost impossible to fire an Israeli worker or move him without his permission and wage increase. On the other hand an Arab worker is exceptionally mobile, he can be fired without notice and moved from one place to another. They don't go on strike, they don't make demands."

When Palestinian workers have raised their heads, the consequences have been historic. The First Intifada (literally "uprising") marks a turning point that underscores the deep connection between economic dependence, labor relations, and ultimately exploitation. In December 1987, an Israeli truck hit a vehicle carrying Palestinian workers in Gaza's Jabalia refugee camp, killing four. The tragic event triggered an unofficial national strike. More than one hundred thousand Palestinian workers boycotted work in Israel, which led to a dramatic halt in production, paralyzing entire sectors of the Israeli economy, especially construction. In response, Israel began to reduce its reliance on Palestinian labor. Throughout the 1990s, it expanded the recruitment of similarly highly exploitable workers from outside the region, including Romania, Thailand, and the Philippines. The number of non-Palestinian workers in Israel jumped from less than twenty thousand in 1993 to one hundred thousand in 1996. In turn, the Palestinian reserve army swelled.

The result of Israel's policies is severe underdevelopment of the Palestinian economy. In 2022, unemployment in the Gaza Strip reached 46 percent, with 63 percent of the population experiencing food insecurity and 80 percent dependent on aid. This is astounding for a region that is just twenty-five miles long with nearly half of its inhabitants under the age of fourteen.

In retaliation for the election of Hamas in 2006, Israel reinforced its economic dominance with military force, imposing a complete blockade on the movement of goods and people in and out of the Gaza Strip. Israel completed the forty-mile high-tech barrier along the entire border with Gaza in late 2021, at a cost of $1.11 billion. *Haaretz* described the wall as "a complex engineering and technological system: the only one of its kind in the world." For a region that Human Rights Watch called "an open-air prison" in 2022, economic development has been an illusion. Even before the genocide that began in the fall of 2023, Israel had banned virtually all exports from Gaza, destroyed its airport, and restricted humanitarian aid to the bare minimum. Today, the region is a brutal killing field—hell on earth.

As of July 2025, official figures state that over seventeen thousand children have been killed in Gaza—an average of twenty-eight per day for more than two years. In the words of UNICEF Executive Director Catherine Russell: "Consider that for a moment. A whole classroom of children killed, every day for nearly two years. . . . They are being killed and maimed as they line up for lifesaving food and medicine."

All the while, no one can escape the politically engineered famine that is tearing through the civilian population, as lifesaving aid trucks remain stalled at the borders, blocked from entering.

Before workers from Gaza and the West Bank were banned from crossing the border with Israel in 2023, the level of surveillance kept intensifying. As was the case in South Africa during the apartheid era, Palestinians were allowed to work only for the employer indicated on their permit—containing both worker and employer details. They were allowed to travel only to the area of their work and were required to return within a certain time or risk arrest. The permits are biometric cards needed to pass through crowded checkpoints, a sector that is very profitable for artificial intelligence corporations that implement automatic facial recognition technology. For decades, the Palestinians have been the most surveilled population in the world, monitored regardless of age, location, or intent.

In his extraordinary book, *The Palestine Laboratory*, investigative journalist Antony Loewenstein uncovered how Israel has monetized its tools of occupation. Starting in the 1990s, the Israeli government imposed austerity on its own population, privatizing vast sectors, including military production, and defunding social spending in favor of heavy subsidies to companies that were developing military surveillance tools. These policies transformed Israel into one of the world's leading tech developers, especially in weapons, surveillance, and cybersecurity. "Cyber is a great business," Prime Minister Benjamin Netanyahu told Tel Aviv University's seventh annual cybersecurity conference in 2017. "It's growing geometrically because there is never a permanent solution, it's a never-ending business."

Israeli corporations are the most competitive in the field, able to market their commodities as being "tested on the Palestinians." While the European Union uses its Heron drones to defend its maritime borders against migrants, Israel's military-industrial complex armed a number of authoritarian governments that perpetuated genocides—against the Tutsi in Rwanda, against the Tamils in Sri Lanka, and against the Rohingya in Myanmar. Most recently, commercial gains have come from selling arms and surveillance tools to the Modi government, supporting its effort to repress the Muslim minority in India, especially in Kashmir, which has become the most militarized region in the world.

While Israeli companies profit, the Palestinian people die. Israeli military operations following the events of October 7, 2023, have bulldozed all of Gaza's already weak productive infrastructure, along with almost all homes, hospitals, and schools. The ground itself is so polluted that even subsistence-level agriculture will be impossible for years to come. The few surviving Palestinians will be left with no choice but to plead for aid from the very countries that have profited from the development and sale of the advanced military technology that killed their children.

The relationship of Israel with the Palestinian territories vividly illustrates how the capitalist wealth of developed nations is built on the subjugation of weaker economies. Some mechanisms of this subjugation appear impersonal, like the imposition of free market policies or fiscal austerity; others are overtly political, like the colonial confiscation of land. Historically, the two have gone hand in hand. In the case of Israel, the inherent violence of capital accumulation has morphed into something extreme.

The merciless fate of the Palestinian people is a magnifying lens that allows us to clearly see the true nature of the socioeconomic system we have constructed. It puts into focus the inverted essence of our society, in which monetary value prevails over all other principles. The ongoing genocide—which the UN commission called a crime against humanity, that of extermination—is inseparable from the economic incentive of higher profits: from buoyant stocks in the weapons industry, to plans for lucrative reconstruction projects, to control over natural resources and commerce in a strategic region. Even as they sponsor lavish philanthropic galas, America's biggest banks are cashing in on the destruction of human life. Goldman Sachs and Bank of America have poured $7.2 billion and $3.5 billion respectively into Israeli "war bonds"—profiting off the massacre of starving Palestinians. Western media compounds this physical violence with epistemic violence, systematically erasing the truth of daily death involving doctors, teachers, journalists, and children—denying them even their most basic humanity. This is not an exception but a stark amplification of the same logic that defines mainstream economics: obscuring reality instead of explaining it, and leaving us powerless in the face of the pursuit of profit.

Class Perspective Now

We should not fall into the trap of focusing on national interests and geopolitical conflicts at the expense of a class perspective. While it is true that some nations benefit from globalized capitalism more than others, and that this globalization is not natural but the result of political decisions with a colonial history, it is equally important to note that the very concept of national unity is a falsehood. Even in the richest economies, people's suffering persists. Israel is among the most unequal developed nations in the world, with its working class bearing the brunt of capitalist austerity. Nearly two million Israelis, about twenty percent of the population, live below the poverty line, including almost one-third of the country's children. And even within the most fragile countries, the elites reap enormous benefits from the status quo of dependency that they collaborate to maintain. In the case of Palestine, for instance, when Israel banned trade relations between the West Bank and Gaza in 1967, Palestinian merchant capitalists acquired licenses to market Israeli products, aligning their economic interests with the occupiers'. Because of the increased trade with Israel, their businesses flourished.

In the international economic hierarchy, local elites in the Global South also benefit from austerity policies. When the Federal Reserve decides to raise interest rates to combat inflation, striking down the American working class, the ripples of monetary austerity are felt internationally. Certainly, international creditors of the Global North benefit from the higher interest rates that countries indebted in US dollars have to pay. But local capital holders also benefit, since central banks in the Global South will raise their own interest rates to prevent investors, attracted by higher returns, from moving their capital to the US.

Such cases are countless. South Africa spends over 21 percent of its revenue on debt payments. If its creditors were to raise interest rates by one percentage point, the country would owe an extra 7.3 billion rand (over 4 billion US dollars). The state spends 30 percent more on debt interest payments than on health care. As the most unequal country in the world, South Africa has never fully escaped the shadow of apartheid. Austerity policies continue to deprive the Black working populations of basic rights, including mobility, as costly private transportation limits access to the city.

In June 2023 the Brazilian Central Bank set interest rates at 13.75 percent, and the wealthy private holders of governmental debt, just 10 percent of society, reaped all the advantages. National and international creditors gained around 700 billion reals (over 1 billion US dollars, equivalent to 7 percent of Brazil's GDP) in one year. The Brazilian state did not incur debt to build schools or fund its social programs. Nevertheless, public debt increased: 82 percent of it resulted from accumulated interest.

As public social services wane, people survive by taking out private loans. Brazilian economist Ladislau Dowbor explains: "It's no wonder that 79 percent of Brazilian households are mired in debt, working to pay interest and often only prolonging the debt. In 2023, 70 million adults are in default, which amounts to a personal bankruptcy crisis on a massive scale." He points out that while the central bank claims to be autonomous, "it is controlled by the very groups it should regulate." Interest payments, combined with tax evasions and tax exemptions, lead to a staggering 30 percent of Brazil's GDP that is transferred from workers to capital holders every year. These figures are a reminder that the public discourse on "financial responsibility" is only a facade.

Perpetual debt is a problem for people but not for our economic system. While creditors get richer, the pressure for more austerity becomes insatiable.

The case of Sri Lanka, an island nation of just under 22 million, offers an especially vivid picture of the voracity of the current global economic system. The country is experiencing a severe economic and financial crisis with disastrous social repercussions, particularly in terms of nutritional security. The

UN World Food Programme reports that one-third of families lack a secure source of food.

Popular protests against an economy that serves very few wealthy individuals reached their peak in July 2022, when about two million demonstrators occupied the government's offices, forcing President Gotabaya Rajapaksa to flee and resign. With his successor, President Ranil Wickremesinghe, the austerity counteroffensive was swift under the suffocating pressure of the International Monetary Fund. A country reeling from the foreign debt default in April 2022 succumbed to an austerity plan according to the usual mechanisms.

Fiscal austerity took the form of cuts to social spending; the elimination of subsidies on essential goods such as gasoline and electricity; regressive taxation, including an increase in taxes on cigarettes, liquor, and telecommunications; and the extension of taxes to low-income households who had been exempt. Monetary austerity, in the form of raising interest rates, exacerbated an already dire situation of unemployment and job insecurity and led to a recession.

Austerity might seem counterproductive. These contractionary measures tend to suppress growth rather than stimulate it. How is it possible that the IMF proposes it again and again as the only solution? Everything makes sense if we abandon the belief that the global capitalist economy works for the good of all. Our economic system requires and thus prioritizes this one-sided class war.

As always, the blame for monetary imbalance is placed on the improper behavior of the people, who supposedly consume too much. Thus, the key to curbing inflation and restoring the value of the Sri Lankan rupee is to suppress internal demand, thereby limiting imports and improving the balance of payments. In simple terms, it is necessary to repress the purchasing power of the majority of citizens. The stability of the internal and external currency is then achieved at the expense of the population, who literally starves. In this way our economic system tends to devour those who are the very source of value on which the system feeds, acting, in the adverb of Nancy Fraser, "cannibalistically."

Capitalism has no vision for humanity. There are another fifty countries in the Global South experiencing debt problems. Structural poverty fills the boats of migrants who try to cross the Mediterranean in search of a livelihood, maybe even a happy life. And a reasonable prediction is that there will be 1.2 billion climate refugees by 2050. The wealthy European states react with the militarization of their borders, a great opportunity for private investors. According to Antony Loewenstein, from 2015 to 2023 the EU spent at least $3.7 billion on high-tech research to find the most efficient ways to target migrants. The same corporations that make profits out of everlasting wars, such as Airbus, BAE Systems, and Leonardo, then sell their drones to keep displaced people out. The Mediterranean region is a deadly area where, according to the International Organization for Migration's Missing Migrants Project, at least 31,206 people died from 2014 to 2024, including at least 1,328 children. The US protects its border with Mexico with lethal technology, paying millions to at least thirteen military companies including Elbit, Lockheed Martin, Raytheon, and General Dynamics.

It is time to demand an economic system that does not flourish at the expense of humanity.

5.

DEMOCRACY IS ANTI-CAPITALISM

In a letter written in 1926, Montagu Norman, the technocratic governor of the Bank of England, expressed distrust for Mussolini's fascist regime, which was killing political opponents and curtailing freedom of expression. However, even Norman had to admit that it was the best option to avoid dangerous anti-capitalist outcomes: "Fascism has surely brought order out of chaos over the last few years: something of the kind was no doubt needed if the pendulum was not to swing too far in quite the other direction. Il Duce was the right man at a critical moment." These thoughts, written at a time when Mussolini's repressive state apparatus had been perfected, were addressed to his friend and colleague Jack Morgan Jr., the owner of J. P. Morgan and Co., which provided vital financial support to Mussolini's dictatorship and remains the most powerful bank in the United States today.

Most of us share the conviction that liberalism and fascism are worlds apart, both ideologically and institutionally. Liberalism values individual rights, while fascism prioritizes the national "whole"; liberalism supports checks and balances in government, while fascism has historically led to concentrated power. However, if we look closely at each camp's economic policies, this belief might shatter, and today's supposedly democratic economic and political institutions appear very differently.

Mussolini's fascist regime was not the result of a coup d'état that seized power through violence. Rather, it was the result of a pernicious process in which bourgeois and liberal government bodies handed over power, knowing they couldn't manage the existential crisis of capitalism in any other way. After the "terror" caused by workers' self-governance, which had depressed the currency's international rating, with a significant depreciation of the lira, all eyes turned to Mussolini. British newspaper *The Times* enthusiastically welcomed "a government against waste" and applauded his minister of economics, Alberto De' Stefani, as the equivalent of an "Oxford Don," a professor whose collaborators were "soaked in English economic thought" and who was resolutely determined to break strikes and foster private investment. Liberals and fascists shared the common goal of protecting the capital order and aligned on the method to do so: aggressive austerity policies.

It is common among well-meaning liberals to point fingers at the likes of Donald Trump, Viktor Orbán, and Giorgia Meloni as bad actors. But the strong parallels between the economic policies of Mussolini's fascist regime and the British government of the 1920s dissolves the reassuring distinction between right-wing authoritarian governments and liberal democracy. This blurred distinction is more common than we might think in the recent history of capitalism.

Throughout the twentieth and twenty-first centuries, economic experts and the liberal establishment have embraced authoritarian governments in the name of economic stability. The most jarring example is Augusto Pinochet's military dictatorship in Chile, ushered in by the bombing of the Palacio de la Moneda on September 11, 1973, to overthrow Salvador Allende, the elected socialist president, who was enabling large-scale redistribution in favor of the working class through the nationalization of key industries previously in the hands of international investors, and land reform that expropriated large estate owners (or *latifundistas*) in favor of landless peasants. The coup, backed by the CIA, paved the way for the "Chicago Boys"—a group of Chilean economists trained at the University of Chicago by neoclassical economists Milton Friedman and Arnold Harberger—to implement their aggressive austerity plan, El Ladrillo (The Brick). This plan privatized the pension system and the bulk of state-owned companies (including banks, utilities, and industries), attacked unions and other labor protections, slashed social expenditures, cut taxes on the wealthy, and increased interest rates. El Ladrillo suppressed the Chilean alternative to capitalism and reduced half the population to poverty.

Pinochet's dictatorship killed, tortured, and detained over forty thousand people. When asked about these events in 2015,

Chilean economist Rolf Lüders, a Chicago Boy and Pinochet's finance minister, reasoned that the regime's political coercion was necessary to carry out their austerity plan: "And if you ask me if you justify the human rights violations? No, I find them awful. But it seems to me that it would not have been possible to make the change that was made in Chile without an authoritarian regime."

The convergence of authoritarianism, economic expertise, and austerity to violate human rights is a recurring theme in modern history. Consider the dramatic support of the liberal world for the authoritarian rule of Boris Yeltsin in Russia. After playing a prominent role in the dissolution of the Soviet Union, Yeltsin pledged to abide by the prescriptions of IMF experts who demanded harsh austerity to transition Russia to a capitalist, market-based economy. Popular opinion soon turned against this austere "shock therapy," and when the Russian parliament challenged these policies and Yeltsin's executive power, violence prevailed over democracy. In the name of economic stability, in October 1993, Yeltsin deployed tanks, helicopters, and soldiers to attack the Russian parliament. The result was hundreds of civilian deaths and injuries. He dissolved the parliament, suspended the constitution, disbanded the constitutional court, shut down newspapers, and jailed his political opponents. *The Economist* had no reservations in endorsing Yeltsin's strongman tactics as necessary to ensure the capital order: "Mr. Yeltsin had to choose between smashing his rival with force or seeing himself, his government, and any prospect of reform destroyed. The threat, in the end, was extreme—

and so, necessarily, was the response." The article concluded, "These gains—the restoration of Mr. Yeltsin's power to govern and renewed progress in economic reform—are great indeed."

While *The Economist* praised the rapid privatization of Russian industries, in the months that followed, a small group of citizens appropriated obscene amounts of national wealth—the infamous Russian oligarchs—while unemployment reached double digits. In 1988, only 2 percent of Russians lived in poverty; by 1995, that number had soared to 50 percent, meaning half the Russian population had become destitute. During the same period, nonwage income (primarily dividends, interests, and entrepreneurial income) rose from 5 percent to 23 percent of GDP.

These immediate and devastating effects of austerity were no surprise. But they were irrelevant to the economists' consensus. Lawrence Summers, then a treasury official in Bill Clinton's administration and a firm supporter of said consensus, insisted that for Russia, "the three '-ations'—privatization, stabilization, and liberalization—must all be completed as soon as possible. Maintaining the momentum of reform is a crucial political problem." The US Congress, keen to address this crucial problem, provided billions in aid to help Yeltsin implement his reforms. The United States Agency for International Development generously funded the Harvard Center for International Development to advise on Yeltsin's austerity program and sent teams of young economists to guide the process. The impact of these "Harvard Boys" in restructuring the Russian economy has lasted for decades.

Capitalism Versus Democracy

It is a stark truth: capitalism and democracy are fundamentally incompatible. While democratic governments, with elections and separation of powers, are a feature of capitalist societies, our understanding of democracy as one based on electoral processes is incomplete. Real democracy requires a modicum of economic agency, which the majority of people don't have.

At the surface level, our capitalist economy has developed hand in hand with electoral democracy. The latter embodies the peculiar—we might say "absurd"—separation between political freedom and economic freedom that is typical of a capitalist society. The legitimacy of the electoral system, accompanied by party pluralism, is a fundamental means by which the capitalist state maintains consensus: it provides us with the illusion of actually having a say over social possibilities. The achievement of universal suffrage gives the impression of having the collective power to decide the future of our country.

After all, we can vote the current government out of office and replace it with another that seems better and, above all, different. The assertion of differences between parties is undoubtedly crucial for the legitimacy of our political system, as it suggests that voters, by voting for competing parties, are choosing between distinct alternatives. However, political sociologist Ralph Miliband's seminal book on Western democracies after World War II challenged this belief. *The State in Capitalist Society* unmasks the fiction in which the tradition of modern democratic liberalism is rooted: the idea that there can be substantially different approaches to managing our economy.

All the parties that govern us, regardless of their political leanings, accept the capitalist context in which they operate as an indisputable premise. Even the Italian Communist Party and the British Labour Party have championed austerity policies at many critical junctures in history. We are therefore talking about a consensus that transcends ideologies and parties, which is embraced even by those considered to be on the side of workers. A powerful passage from Miliband's book:

> What is really striking about these political leaders and political office-holders, in relation to each other, is not their many differences, but the extent of their agreement on truly fundamental issues. . . . Differences and controversies, even at their most intense, have never been allowed by the politicians concerned to bring into question the validity of the "free enterprise" system itself . . . To a much larger extent than appearance and rhetoric have been made to suggest, the politics of advanced capitalism have been about different conceptions of how to run the same economic and social system, and not about radically different social systems.

Before a party can even come close to governing, it usually goes through a process of political education in which it internalizes capitalism's "economic necessities" and adapts to them. Indeed, once the compromise of a society based on wage labor is accepted, the party must adopt policies that maintain a docile labor force and protect profits, essential elements to attract capital investment. What measure of a government's success is greater than having "revived the economy" and gained the trust of the markets?

This means that the essential condition of good governance is to ensure the best general conditions for capital accumulation. Indeed, the very functioning of the state machinery depends on taxes and loans: the results of capital accumulation.

The state, then, in a capitalist society, takes on a specific role: it becomes a spokesperson for the "general interest"—not of any particular capitalist but of the entire economy, an economy that generates value from the exploitation of the majority. And of course, once the working classes are bound by market dependence, they also hope for the economy to do well, so as to secure their jobs. As Miliband explains, governments justify their support of the capitalist class by claiming their pro-business policies are in the national interest and thus benefit everyone:

> Given their view of that system, it is easy to understand why governments should wish to help business in every possible way, yet do not at all feel that this entails any degree of bias towards particular classes, interests and groups. . . . The much-derided phrase "What is good for General Motors is good for America" is only defective in that it tends to identify the interests of one particular enterprise with the national interest. But if General Motors is taken to stand for the world of capitalist enterprise as a whole, the slogan is one to which governments in capital-

ist countries do subscribe, often explicitly. And they do so because they accept the notion that the economic rationality of the capitalist system is synonymous with rationality itself, and that it provides the best possible set of human arrangements in a necessarily imperfect world.

When people question capitalism's rationality, even through democratic means, it frightens the economic experts in power, who fear any potential interference in macroeconomic management that may hamper the capital order. In 1920, Maffeo Pantaleoni actively supported Mussolini's fascist regime out of the conviction that the problem with political democracy was that people did not understand what was in their best interests; they had to be kept away from economic decisions for their own good. He expressed this view at the Brussels conference: "Where Socialism is strong, where democracy is strong, public finance will go the wrong way."

The antidemocratic impulse of the economists in the 1920s has not disappeared; on the contrary, it continues to be reinforced by peer-reviewed scientific publications. Through a burgeoning literature that has been steadily enriched since the 1980s, many economists have promoted the theory that electoral democracies, especially those with proportional representation, have an intrinsic tendency to accumulate debt and thus are economically inefficient. In the words of economist Vittorio Grilli, who played a central role in implementing Italy's austerity plan in the 2010s, "Lack of fiscal discipline is almost exclusively found in countries governed by representational democracies."

The terrible realization is that these economists are not simply wrong. It is true that social demands may endanger economic priorities. Social redistribution risks tilting power relations too much in favor of the working class. For example, if people were able to pressure their governments into providing a dignified basic income, workers would no longer need to submit to the coercion of wage labor; profits, the engine of capitalist economic growth, would decline as businesses would have to raise wages to attract workers who might otherwise leave the workforce. For our system to function optimally, citizens must be excluded from decisions regarding society's production and distribution of resources. It is thus profoundly antidemocratic.

Economic institutions, therefore, are designed to erect the highest possible barriers to economic decision-making. We see a persistent tendency to shield economic governance from public deliberation. In liberal democracies, experts protect their exclusive power to tweak the dials of macroeconomic management by concealing them from popular view. These strategies are so successful that we do not even notice them. Central banks are often insulated with independent status. This institutional construction is accepted without question, but we must recognize that technocratic elites intensified this independence precisely at a moment when the people demanded to participate in monetary and fiscal policies. In the case of the post–World War I period, the experts gathered in Brussels and Genoa faced a practical problem: How could they implement deflationary policies contrary to the interests and sensibilities of the majority?

The solution was to legitimize central banks as independent bodies—"free from political pressures"—to ensure that they were "managed exclusively according to lines dictated by financial prudence." The influential British Treasury economist Ralph Hawtrey openly supported the establishment of a central bank with minimal democratic scrutiny, which could follow the precept "Never explain, never regret, never apologize." The British technocrats exported this model to their colonies and other countries of the Global South, such as Brazil and India.

Today, the tone has not changed. Scientific articles laud the "social desirability" of keeping citizens away from monetary decisions in favor of "an agent whose preferences are more inflation averse than are society's preferences." The policies of central banks are shaped by small groups of experts, an oligarchy of knowledge, founded on pseudoscience. Their exclusive knowledge is the tool used to justify the undemocratic nature of an institution endowed with immense power, capable of influencing the lives of every citizen, from the cost of their cereal to their job opportunities. The European Central Bank retains formal "independence from elected officials," so as to operate "without prejudice" in favor of price stability—its primary mandate. It "explicitly forbids" the bank's board to "receive any instruction from either community or national political institutions." Political independence is accompanied by economic independence: the European Central Bank has no obligation to finance member nations' public deficits, thus heavily restricting social expenditures within its states.

The Federal Reserve of the United States, founded in 1913, is widely considered one of the most autonomous central banks in the world. Its independence was established during the New Deal through the Acts of 1933 and 1935, which granted it full macroeconomic management powers and insulated it from electoral pressures by removing the Treasury secretary and comptroller of the currency—both political appointees—from the Federal Reserve Board of Governors. This autonomy was reinforced by the 1951 Treasury-Fed Accord, which separated monetary policy from congressional control and imposed significant restraints on government spending.

As a state institution exempt from democratic oversight, the Fed exercises full power over monetary policy, prioritizing inflation control over social redistribution. Since the 1980s, the Fed's power has continued to grow, reaching unprecedented levels during the COVID-19 crisis. At that time, the Fed claimed the authority to lend unlimited funds to industrial corporations, regardless of their creditworthiness, effectively risk-proofing their debt and blurring the distinction between public and private debt. Indeed, large corporations did very well: The Fed purchased corporate debt from massive companies, and the federal government initiated the Paycheck Protection Program, which, while targeted at small businesses, ended up lending $1 billion to publicly traded companies, including airlines, cruise companies, and hotel chains. Once again, we see the state shifting resources in favor of capital holders while spreading the costs to everyone else. This is problematic to us as citizens, but it is the key to promoting a healthy environment for capital accumulation.

The antidemocratic structures of economic institutions certainly do not stop at central banks. Since the 1992 Maastricht Treaty, the European Union has embraced austerity policies and empowered technocrats to propose institutional reforms that undermine democracy. Our contemporaries call for electoral reforms aimed at reducing proportional representation (to favor stronger governments) and rewriting the constitutions of local and national governments to include the obligation of a balanced budget. Italy, like many other countries, passed both recommendations in the 2010s, removing the political guardrails that were erected to mark the distance from its fascist past.

"From Citizen to Producer"

In the summer of 2023, at the meeting of the Fórum Internacional Tributário (International Tax Forum) in Brazil, I was on a panel with Amitabh Behar, executive director of Oxfam International, a nonprofit that is a significant source for economic data on inequality. He spoke about Antilia, a residence valued at approximately $4.6 billion that belongs to the richest man in India. Located in Mumbai, Antilia has twenty-seven floors, nine high-speed elevators, a multistory garage that can accommodate 168 cars, three helipads, a large ballroom, a theater, a spa, a temple, and numerous terraced gardens.

In the same city, more than forty thousand children live on the streets, many of whom go hungry and suffer from curable diseases. Before the 2023 G20 summit in New Delhi, the local administration carried out a large-scale "clean-up" and erected high fences around the slums in order to hide the living conditions of the workers who produce value for the global economy. In Mumbai's Dharavi, the largest slum in the world, it is estimated that two million workers generate over $2 billion in wealth, most of which ends up in the bank accounts of large American shareholders. This vast inequality illustrates the deep contradictions of our capitalist economy that must be fought.

The first step toward change is to lay bare that what counts as a social failure is not at all a failure for the logic of capital. To fight this inhumane logic that organizes our society, we must abandon the mystifying language of neoclassical economics in favor of a simple but profound explanation of our economic system, which can shake our beliefs and spur us into action.

What would happen if the majority of people realized that in the last three years, about two-thirds of the wealth created has gone into the hands of 1 percent of the global population? And that while more than 820 million people go to bed with empty stomachs every night, 2,600 billionaires add $2.7 billion to their wealth every day? What if the majority learned that the soap we buy with our wages comes from the Indian Unique Chemicals, a company for which the workers of Dharavi work twelve hours a day for about $70 a month? What if we acknowledged that it is not exceptional greed but the structure of our economic system that fuels these inequalities? These scenarios cannot be classified as "market failures," as economists often do; they are "market successes." Markets only enable the accumulation of ever more capital. We ourselves and the environment that sustains us are mere instruments.

We have created a socioeconomic system in which meeting our needs depends on mechanisms that thrive on their suppression. A far cry from the best possible world, ours is an upside-down one. The genocide in Gaza and the destruction of our ecosystem are tragic products of this glaring truth. As hospitals and schools burn with children inside, international shareholders toast, and the economy grows. From October 2023 to July 2025, the stock price of the two aerospace and defense giants RTX Corporation and Leonardo soared by 77 percent and 234 percent, respectively. In 2023, the revenue of the world's top one hundred arms companies sat at over $600 billion. The whole economy is implicated. In her extraordinary June 2025 UN report, Special Rapporteur Francesca Albanese exposes a network of enablers that sustain the arms industry's windfall, including law firms, auditing and consulting firms, arms dealers, universities, and brokers. She unveils the vast web of corporations and intermediaries for whom the destruction of Palestinian life has translated into record profits—for tech giants like Alphabet, Microsoft, and Amazon, financial powerhouses such as Vanguard and BlackRock, and the world's largest extractive and energy conglomerates.

While investing in social programs that support a dignified life risks challenging the class structure, military spending is very much compatible with the requirements of our capitalist economy. Militarism is necessary to capital accumulation because it solves the enduring problem of overproduction. Companies frequently produce more goods than workers can afford. Austerity measures keep most people's purchasing power depleted, limiting their spending and the economy's growth. However, the state's perennial demand for bombs and other military instruments ensures sustained economic expansion, perfectly serving the system—in an awful, inhuman way. A 1959 cost-benefit analysis of defense spending by US government officials summarized this dynamic in telling language: costs equal "lives or physical injuries"; benefits equal "growth-stimulating effects on the economy."

In the meantime, prolonged droughts, more frequent floods, life-threatening heat waves, fires, and desertification haven't yet stopped fossil fuel and gas extraction from increasing every year. Although the richest 10 percent of the global population is responsible for half of all carbon dioxide emissions, it is overwhelmingly the poor in the Global South who die from resulting natural disasters.

I am often pressed with the question "So, what do you suggest? Revolution?" In our imagination, the term "revolution" is associated with something bloody, barbaric, and wrong. But it shouldn't have to be. Others say, "Face it, haven't we tried everything already? Look at Soviet Russia and China!" These retorts propose false alternatives that support the dominant narrative, as they offer examples of societies that have not managed to overcome the coercion of global market competition, exploitation, and hierarchical divisions. Let's free ourselves from these mental traps.

Historical change does not happen out of blueprints; alternatives develop through peoples' active participation, and it is only if we have the conceptual tools to understand the world differently that we can act differently. I cherish Antonio Gramsci's intuition that the combination of knowledge that is at once theoretical and practical can guide us toward new horizons, provided that we engage personally and concretely. As radical historian Robin Kelley puts it, "Revolutionary dreams erupt out of political engagement; collective social movements are incubators of new knowledge." New knowledge entails collective self-transformation.

Each of us can take steps to politicize our lives. And by "politicize," I mean participate in the transformation of the material and social reality around us. The steps can be as small as connecting with your neighbors to build community. After all, getting to know your neighbors is typically the first step in starting initiatives to stand up for basic resources, such as tenant organizations to protect renters' rights or community food programs. If you're a student, you might stand up for your fellow student workers or organize assemblies to oppose your university's investment in corporations that profit off human rights violations. In my own efforts, here in Tulsa, Oklahoma, at the Forum for Humane Economics (FREE), we hold monthly discussions with citizens from all walks of life to connect our daily problems to the economic structures that create them and envisage courageous alternatives. The Forum is structured as a council and is the product of a collective endeavor to spread economic knowledge, both locally and internationally, that fortifies the organization of effective systems of economic solidarity. It connects existing realities on the ground, such as Cooperation Tulsa, which, inspired by Cooperation Jackson in Mississippi, collectively owns and organizes the production and distribution of food in a peripheral urban setting, and the Really Really Free Market, which organizes the exchange of essential goods without the intermediation of money. The path toward concrete transformation begins with real connections and conversations.

Challenging austerity capitalism means voting against and protesting cuts to public health programs and schools as well as the use of our tax money to finance unending wars. It also means playing offense: pressuring politicians to tax the rich and to enact radical public programs—like social housing and governmental support for workers' cooperatives—that challenge the logic of profit and growth. However, we must remember that to every degree that these reforms challenge the capital order, so long as we stay within this order, the capitalist class will attack them. Indeed, we cannot see reforms like universal health care as the end goal. Mobilizing for reforms can certainly spread awareness about how the system operates and build collective strength. If won, reforms can provide greater strength, time, and resources to fight, but we must keep pushing for a society that is based on different principles.

That's why radical strategies are needed too. We have to take back the ability to collectively decide what and how much we want to produce, what energy sources to rely on, and how to structure power relations in the workplace. We have to take back command over production and our relationship with nature, and we must make decisions with the well-being of future generations in mind.

The world is brimming with collective organizations that defy the logic of our economic system, that puncture the capital order, and that push society to reimagine its foundations. In summer 2024, I learned about Comuna da Terra Irmã Alberta, an agroecological commune sprawling over 270 acres on the outskirts of São Paulo, Brazil. It was founded in 2002 by a group of poor families who mobilized to reclaim unused land from the São Paulo State Basic Sanitation Company, which planned to turn it into a landfill.

Comuna da Terra Irmã Alberta symbolizes a new economic model: sixty-four formerly destitute families practice self-managed sustainable agriculture there. These families learned sophisticated agroforestry techniques through a community-wide program. After clearing the land, they cultivated the soil into large collective areas, planting beans and native trees. The environmental impacts have been significant: they restored seven water springs, preserved a depleted aquifer, and brought back wildlife that had vanished due to vegetation degradation. The community's approach to organizing production is closely intertwined with its cultural-political projects. The commune's cultural institution, Okaracy Cultural Territory, collaborates with a self-organized theater company, Antropofagica, which uses theater and art to boost collective consciousness, especially among youths.

Comuna de Terra Irmã Alberta faces constant battles for recognition, having received multiple eviction orders, especially after the early 2000s, when private investors accrued almost half the sanitation company's shares. But it is evidence that when people build a democratic means of subsistence, they can regain power and freedom. The commune's contrast with its surroundings is stark: next to the community's reclaimed land, the company Minalba has installed a mineral-water bottling plant, turning pure water from the aquifer into a commodity for those who can afford it.

From the beginning, Comuna da Terra Irmã Alberta has been part of a broader network fighting for a new economic model:

the Movimento dos Trabalhadores Rurais Sem Terra (MST), or Landless Workers' Movement. Founded in 1984, MST is one of the world's largest land movements, with over 1.5 million members across twenty-three of Brazil's twenty-six states.

MST operates on two interconnected fronts. First, on the legal front, it demands that the Brazilian government enforce an article in its constitution that requires rural property to be seized and redistributed if it fails to serve a social function. MST's goal is to use the legal system to push the capitalist state to prioritize values beyond austerity and capital accumulation. At the same time, the movement has proposed entirely different objectives for the land it has secured. For example, MST aims to achieve popular food sovereignty—community control over how food is produced and distributed—and to combat the concentration of land in a few hands. This means opposing agribusinesses focused on exports that devastate ecosystems and create the dystopian reality of 33 million people going hungry in one of the world's largest food-producing countries. This mission requires rethinking the very social relations of production, transforming laborers exploited by large agribusinesses into communal owners who self-manage sustainable agriculture practices.

MST's strategy merges economic and political organization and strives to achieve horizontal representation, much like the Turin council model of Gramsci discussed in chapter 2. The basic organizational unit, the "nucleo de base," consists of ten to fifteen families living in MST encampments or settlements. Each unit identifies and addresses issues faced by its member families, such as access to education or health care, and elects two representatives, one woman and one man, to attend settlement and encampment assemblies. These representatives participate in regional meetings, where they elect regional representatives who, in turn, choose members of the MST's state coordinating body and national coordinating bodies. The representatives of MST function as spokespeople who are recallable by and accountable to their base. This means that if a representative is perceived as failing to fulfill their responsibilities, acting contrary to the collective interest, or not adhering to the principles of the movement, they can be replaced through a democratic process. MST's grassroots, decentralized political organization models how to actively involve people in the material decisions that shape their lives.

Victories are concrete: more than 450,000 families have gained legal access to land. MST is at the cutting edge of agroecology, producing its own bio-fertilizers that reduce dependence on industrial chemicals. For ten years now, MST has been the biggest producer of organic rice in Latin America. MST also partners with public universities to develop technology for its solidarity economy. For example, farmers have worked closely with Professor Celso Alexandre Souza de Alvear from Federal University of Rio de Janeiro to create several software programs that help MST farming collectives plan production and distribute their produce.

Leaders of these movements recognize that the fight for a postcapitalist alternative must be global and interconnected. La Via Campesina, an international farmers' organization founded in Belgium in 1993, is one such channel, building a network of 182 organizations across eighty-one countries.

The rural front for a postcapitalist world has its urban counterpart in Brazil: the Movimento dos Trabalhadores Sem Teto (MTST), or Homeless Workers' Movement, which occupies vacant buildings and pressures the government to fulfill the constitutional right to housing. Its demands are a reaction to skyrocketing homelessness in Brazil, where over 80 percent of unhoused workers are Black. The housing crisis has been exacerbated by the government's prioritization of attracting investments in large infrastructure projects for events like the World Cup over apartments that address urgent needs.

According to MST leader João Pedro Stédile, the urban crisis highlights the necessity for a complete overhaul of our economic model. "People are living a hell in the big cities," he says, "losing three, four hours a day in transit when they could be with family, studying, or involved in cultural activities." The MTST aims to decommodify housing, food, and social life: its self-managed residences become hubs for solidarity kitchens, largely led by Black women, who foster care and political recognition. Its research center, alongside the MST's national school, affirms how knowledge should not be confined to academics in privileged settings but created by thinkers whose lived experience informs their struggle for a democratic economic system.

Meanwhile, workers operate more than fifty self-managed factories in Brazil and four hundred factories in Argentina. These are spaces that workers took over after their owners had decided to relocate or to shut them down. The idea that private capital is essential for production and investment is a myth.

Alternatives to private investment are real, from collective ownership by workers to public investment. In fact, public investment has historically been at the heart of major technological advancement, and public investment can be made accountable to democratic control. Governments that have the courage to break with the logic of capitalism can empower workers' initiatives. For example, the government of Mexican President Claudia Sheinbaum is reasserting the priority of housing needs over real estate development. Her social housing initiative is mobilizing substantial public resources to build one million new homes and guarantee a right to housing. A key player in this effort is the National Workers' Housing Fund (Infonavit), which will directly construct housing to reduce production costs. This initiative is expected to generate 6.1 million direct jobs and 9.2 million indirect jobs. It specifically targets vulnerable groups, including female heads of households, youths, Indigenous communities, and senior citizens. When asked about the funding, Sheinbaum's response was clear: the money was always there; it just needed to be redirected.

These ambitious national goals advance the work of local officials like Clara Brugada. Elected mayor of Mexico City in October 2024, Brugada is known for spearheading ambitious models of social infrastructure in the borough of Iztapalapa, historically the most deprived area of Mexico City. There, Brugada has built numerous Utopias, community centers that promote sports, culture, and health initiatives and empower people to think ambitiously about their economic rights.

Fires of rebellion are igniting globally. In the summer of 2024, Kenyan youths risked their lives, protesting in the streets against a finance bill that once again put the burden of debt repayment on the lower classes of society. Millions raised their voices in the capital of Nairobi and in over thirty-five Kenyan counties, uniting across ethnic and religious lines to resist a regressive tax program—with new taxes on everyday items such as bread, diapers, and gasoline—introduced to meet the fiscal austerity requirement of Kenya's latest IMF and World Bank loans. Despite brutal state repression, they won, forcing the government to withdraw the program. They showed how grassroots organizations and popular action can effectively challenge capitalist economic principles. The victory in Kenya inspired many other youth-led protests, which have swept sub-Saharan Africa, from Nigeria to Uganda to Mozambique. Deep economic injustices, including the permanent deterioration of social services, inequalities, and skyrocketing youth unemployment are driving a new political movement.

In Palestine, the violent effort to suppress the most basic attempts to safeguard human rights—including the jailing and torture of peaceful marchers hoping to break the food blockade in Gaza and the attack on the Freedom Flotilla led by Greta Thunberg carrying humanitarian aid—attests to the strength of a growing international movement for Palestinian liberation that is threatening exactly because it connects the dots: to escape genocide, we must also escape capitalism. We can all be free only when the most oppressed are free.

A few months after the end of World War I, moral philosopher Zino Zini gave a lecture titled "From Citizen to Producer." He argued that the citizen as commonly viewed in a capitalist democracy is a passive individual, "theoretically sovereign, but in fact, only so on election day; the rest of the time, he is nothing but a subject subordinated to laws and regulations, drafted and promulgated without his actual participation." The citizen lives a political servitude founded on economic servitude: How much do our votes really count when our options are circumscribed by market dependence and wage labor? The inequality of classes within the matrix of production effectively prevents any genuinely democratic relationship between free human beings. Instead, Zini argues, we must become active producers: participating on equal terrain in the construction and change of our social reality.

Zini opposed an abstract, indirect idea of political freedom, arguing that it is impossible without economic freedom. We must reclaim the word "freedom." Our new class lens helps us call out and contradict the guardians of the capital order, who use "freedom" to disguise their defense of the market economy. Economic freedom is really about emancipation from exploitation and impersonal domination. It is freedom from the obsessive and paralyzing centrality of an inhumane economic system. It is freedom to put human value before economic self-interest, to do work that is meaningful for oneself and others. It is the freedom to fully realize our capacities as flourishing, compassionate beings. It is freedom to reconstitute social bonds and solidarities. Economic freedom is true liberation.

ACKNOWLEDGMENTS

This book would not exist without the initial inspiration of my Italian editor, Maurizio Donati, who motivated me to write a broader public intervention after reading my book *The Capital Order* (University of Chicago Press, 2022). The Italian edition, *L'Economia è politica* (Fuori Scena, 2023), indeed forms the basis for this expanded and transformed English version.

The excellent editorial work of Jennie Miller, Hana Teraie-Wood, and Eric Henney has been invaluable in shaping my ideas into a more engaging and coherent form. A special thanks to editor Stephen Morrow, whose passionate belief in the project made it possible. His insightful advice and enthusiastic contributions greatly enhanced the book's structure and flow.

I owe a profound debt of gratitude to my research assistants and brilliant graduate students, Aditya Singh and Iris Graham, who have worked closely with me throughout this journey. Their invaluable insights, expertise, and support—both intellectual and emotional—were crucial in bringing this book to fruition.

My sincere appreciation goes to Professor Ibrahim Shikaki, whose guidance helped me find the appropriate literature and approach for chapter 5. I am also immensely thankful to Professor Duncan Foley for his critical feedback, particularly on chapter 3 addressing unemployment and inflation; his suggestions were, as always, invaluable. A special thank-you to my friends Ritchie Tabachnick and Morris Pearl for their thoughtful reading of the manuscript and their constructive comments. I am grateful to Lauren Johnston, Emma Cahill, and Crys LaCroix for their helpful suggestions in the final round of the edits.

Finally, my husband Federico's unwavering emotional and practical support sustains my work every day. His encouragement and understanding make my endeavors possible, and I am profoundly grateful for his presence in my life.

NOTES

Translations from Italian are the author's own unless otherwise noted.

Introduction: Economics Is a Political Act

1 **"The manual workers":** League of Nations, *Proceedings of the Brussels International Financial Conference, 1920*, vol. 2 of 5, *Verbatim Record of the Debate* (London: Harrison and Sons, 1920–1921), 20.
3 **"act on public opinion":** League of Nations, *Proceedings of the Brussels International Financial Conference*, 2:75 (my italics).
3 **"The factories yesterday evening":** *Corriere della sera* [August 31, 1920], reprinted in Paolo Spriano, *The Occupation of the Factories: Italy 1920* (London: Pluto Press, 1975), 54.
3 **An emblematic photograph:** On the Italian factory occupation, see Clara E. Mattei, "The New Order," chap. 4 in *The Capital Order: How Economists Invented Austerity and Paved the Way to Fascism* (Chicago: University of Chicago Press, 2022), particularly pages 116–22.
4 **"new society of free":** Zino Zini, "Da cittadino a produttore" [From citizen to producer], *L'Ordine nuovo* 1, no. 38 (February 21, 1920): 301–2.
4 **"capitalist system generally":** "Keynes's Note of Interview with Chancellor" (February 15, 1920, T 172/1384), cited in Susan Howson, "'A Dear Money Man'? Keynes on Monetary Policy, 1920," *Economic Journal* 83, no. 330 (1973): 459, https://doi.org/10.2307/2231181.

NOTES

4 **"conspicuous increases in unnecessary consumption":** Luigi Einaudi, *Prediche* (Bari: G. Laterza, 1920): 96–97 (italics in the original).

5 **"live like pigs":** Maffeo Pantaleoni, *Bolcevismo italiano* (Bari: Laterza, 1922): xiv.

5 **"will also bring some pain":** For the declarations of the Fed's president at the annual meeting of central banks, see Jerome H. Powell, "Monetary Policy and Price Stability," August 26, 2022, at Reassessing Constraints on the Economy and Policy, an economic policy symposium sponsored by the Federal Reserve Bank of Kansas City, Jackson Hole, Wyoming, transcript, https://www.federalreserve.gov/newsevents/speech/powell20220826a.htm.

5 **an "unhealthy" or "tight" labor market:** Powell, "Monetary Policy and Price Stability."

6 **"serves as a worker-discipline device":** See the memo by Janet Yellen, "Job Insecurity, the Natural Rate of Unemployment, and the Phillips Curve," written for Alan Greenspan, Board of Governors of the Federal Reserve System, found in Jon Schwarz, "In Confidential Memo, Treasury Secretary Janet Yellen Celebrated Unemployment as a 'Worker-Discipline Device,'" *The Intercept*, January 24, 2023, https://theintercept.com/2023/01/24/unemployment-inflation-janet-yellen/.

6 **"I think the problem":** "Tim Gurner at the AFR Property Summit," summit discussion recording, posted September 15, 2023, by *Financial Review*, YouTube, https://www.youtube.com/watch?v=_K1tqDyN4xE.

8 **the "Great Resignation":** The Great Resignation, a phenomenon characterized by a significant number of US workers quitting their jobs, was particularly pronounced during 2021 and 2022, the initial years of the COVID-19 pandemic. According to the US Bureau of Labor Statistics, tens of millions of workers resigned, leading to substantial labor market shifts; in 2021 alone, about 47.8 million workers quit their jobs, and in 2022, the trend continued, with over 50 million resignations. As of 2023, the total US workforce, which includes both employed and unemployed individuals actively seeking work, stands at approximately 161 million people.

8 **voluntarily leaving their jobs:** Stefan Ellerbeck, "The Great Resignation Continues. Why Are US Workers Continuing to Quit Their Jobs?," World Economic Forum, January 25, 2023, https://www.weforum.org/stories/2023/01/us-workers-jobs-quit/.

9 **the top 0.1 percent owns more than five times:** "Distribution of Household Wealth in the U.S. Since 1989," Federal Reserve, updated March 21, 2025, accessed June 19, 2025, https://www.federalreserve.gov/releases/z1/dataviz/dfa/distribute/table/#quarter:129;series:Net%20worth;demographic:networth;population:all;units:levels.

9 **Since 2014, the number of children living in poverty:** House of Lords Library, "Child Poverty: Statistics, Causes and the UK's Policy

NOTES 169

Response," House of Lords Library, August 2, 2023, https://lordslibrary.parliament.uk/child-poverty-statistics-causes-and-the-uks-policy-response. The 2013–14 stats are from Department for Work and Pensions, "Households Below Average Income: 1994/95 to 2013/14," tables 4a and 4b 2015, https://www.gov.uk/government/statistics/households-below-average-income-19941995-to-20132014.

9 **Globally the superrich saw extraordinary gains:** "Richest 1% Grab Nearly Twice as Much New Wealth as Rest of the World Put Together," press release, Oxfam UK, January 16, 2023, https://www.oxfam.org.uk/media/press-releases/richest-1-grab-nearly-twice-as-much-new-wealth-as-rest-of-the-world-put-together/.

12 **More than half of all Americans live in financial insecurity:** Gregory Acs, Ilham Dehry, Linda Giannarelli, and Margaret Todd, *Measuring the True Cost of Economic Security* (Urban Institute, November 2024), https://www.urban.org/research/publication/measuring-true-cost-economic-security.

17 **she carried messages to her *partigiani* comrades:** Suzanne Cope, "How One Jewish Woman Fought the Nazis—and Helped Found a New Italian Republic," *Forward*, May 10, 2025, https://forward.com/culture/716905/how-one-jewish-woman-fought-the-nazis-and-helped-found-a-new-italian-republic/.

Chapter 1: The Invisible Order

20 **of which more than 44,000 are children:** Coalition for the Homeless, "Facts About Homelessness," November 2024, Coalition for the Homeless, https://www.coalitionforthehomeless.org/facts-about-homelessness/. See also Advocates for Children of New York, "Student Homelessness in New York City, 2023–24," November 18, 2024, https://advocatesforchildren.org/policy-resource/student-homelessness-data-2024/; and Erum Salam, "Record Number of New York City Public School Students Were Homeless Last Year," *The Guardian*, November 18, 2024, https://www.theguardian.com/us-news/2024/nov/18/new-york-city-students-homeless.

20 **over sixty thousand apartments are vacant in New York:** Greg David, "Tens of Thousands of Rent-Stabilized Apartments Remain Off the Market During Record Housing Shortage," *The City*, February 14, 2024, https://www.thecity.nyc/2024/02/14/rent-stabilized-apartments-vacant/.

20 **global elite not to live in but as financial assets:** Quinn Slobodian, *Crack-Up Capitalism: Market Radicals and the Dream of a World Without Democracy* (New York: Metropolitan Books, 2023), 233.

21 **To solve homelessness through housing construction:** See the 2022 report of the nonprofit Corporation for Supportive Housing, *The California Homeless Housing Needs Assessment: $8.1 Billion Every Year.*

That's How We Solve Homelessness, accessed October 21, 2024, https://calneeds.csh.org/. Note that President Joe Biden signed the Fiscal 2023 National Defense Authorization Act into law, allotting $816.7 billion to the Defense Department; see Jim Garamone, "Biden Signs National Defense Authorization Act into Law," US Department of Defense, December 23, 2022, https://www.defense.gov/News/News-Stories/Article/Article/3252968/biden-signs-national-defense-authorization-act-into-law/.

21 **over 800 million people suffer from hunger:** World Health Organization, *Hunger Numbers Stubbornly High for Three Consecutive Years as Global Crises Deepen: UN Report*, July 24, 2024, https://www.who.int/news/item/24-07-2024-hunger-numbers-stubbornly-high-for-three-consecutive-years-as-global-crises-deepen--un-report. Statistics reported from the Food and Agriculture Organization of the United Nations, *The State of Food Security and Nutrition in the World*, 2024, https://openknowledge.fao.org/server/api/core/bitstreams/39dbc6d1-58eb-4aac-bd8a-47a8a2c07c67/content/cd1254en.html#gsc.tab=0.

21 **13.5 percent of households were food insecure in 2023:** Economic Research Service, "Food Security in the U.S.—Key Statistics and Graphics," US Department of Agriculture, updated January 8, 2025, https://www.ers.usda.gov/topics/food-nutrition-assistance/food-security-in-the-us/key-statistics-graphics.

21 **products at or near expiration are discarded:** For more on the topic, see a classic: Raj Patel, *Stuffed and Starved: The Hidden Battle for the World Food System* (Brooklyn: Melville House, 2008).

23 **his influential essay:** Francis Fukuyama, "The End of History?," *The National Interest*, no. 16 (Summer 1989): 3–18.

23 **the very thought of subverting capitalism becomes unthinkable:** For a fundamental book that shows the limits of the dominant literature on the origins of capitalism and proposes an alternative reading, which we have resumed in these pages, see Ellen Meiksins Wood, *The Origin of Capitalism: A Longer View* (London: Verso Books, 2002).

23 **industrial capitalism has existed for less than three hundred years:** Our economic system is the result of a long-term historical process that lasted from the fifteenth to the eighteenth centuries. The literature on this topic is extensive, with opposing positions. See, for example, the so-called Brenner debate, named after the historian Robert Brenner and triggered by his classic article: Robert Brenner, "Agrarian Class Structure and Economic Development in Pre-Industrial Europe," *Past and Present* 70, no. 1 (1976): 30–75, https://academic.oup.com/past/article-abstract/70/1/30/1417447.

23 **The foundational element of capitalism:** In her famous book *The Origin of Capitalism*, Ellen Meiksins Wood boosts Robert Brenner's critique of the so-called New Smithian understanding of the origins of capitalism, which focuses on the expansion of trade and markets rather

than the qualitative change of social relations of production; see Ellen Meiksins Wood, *The Origin of Capitalism* (London: Verso Books, 2017). David McNally argues that the whole new literature, the so-called New History of Capitalism, suffers from the same methodological limitation of focusing on the realm of exchange, which brings about a naturalization of capitalist social relations and the implicit disavowal of the agency of workers; see David McNally, *Slavery and Capitalism: A New Marxist History* (Oakland: University of California Press, 2025), 6–15.

24 **disrupting indigenous economic systems in the process:** Karl Marx, "The Modern Theory of Colonization," chap. 33 in *Capital*, trans. Ben Fowkes, introduction by Ernest Mandel (London: Penguin Classics, 1992). See also Walter Rodney, *How Europe Underdeveloped Africa* (London: Bogle-L'Ouverture, 1972); Eduardo Galeano, *Open Veins of Latin America: Five Centuries of the Pillage of a Continent* (New York: Monthly Review Press, 1997); Ugo Mattei and Laura Nader, *Plunder: When the Rule of Law Is Illegal* (Malden, MA: Blackwell, 2008); and Raj Patel and Jason W. Moore, *A History of the World in Seven Cheap Things: A Guide to Capitalism, Nature, and the Future of the Planet* (Oakland: University of California Press, 2018).

25 **not ownership as we think of it:** Still fundamental for understanding feudalism is Marc Bloch's famous work *La Société féodale* (Paris: Éditions Albin Michel, 1939). See also Maurice Dobb, "Transition from Feudalism to Capitalism," chap. 1 in *Papers on Capitalism, Development and Planning* (New York: International Publishers, 1967).

25 **a tumultuous process of privatization:** For a detailed description of the historical process of primitive accumulation in Britain, please refer to Marx, "Expropriation of the Agricultural Population from the Land," chap. 27 in *Capital*; E. P. Thompson, *The Making of the English Working Class* (New York: Pantheon, 1964); Karl Polanyi, *The Great Transformation: The Political and Economic Origins of Our Time* (Boston: Beacon Press, 2001); and J. L. Hammond and Barbara Hammond, *The Village Labourer* (Stroud: Nonsuch, 2005). For a perspective that problematizes the relationship between female subjugation, wage labor, and capitalism, see Silvia Federici, *Caliban and the Witch* (Brooklyn: Autonomedia, 2004).

25 **less than 30 percent still held in common:** Gregory Clark and Anthony Clark, "Common Rights to Land in England, 1475–1839," *Journal of Economic History* 61, no. 4 (2002): 1009–36.

25 **Parliament passed the Enclosure Acts:** C. Ford Runge and Edi Defrancesco, "Exclusion, Inclusion, and Enclosure: Historical Commons and Modern Intellectual Property," *World Development* 34, no. 10 (2006).

26 **"will be converted into":** Richard Price, *Observations on Reversionary Payments*, 6th ed. (London: 1803), 147, cited in Marx, "The Expropriation of the Agricultural Population from the Land," chap. 27 in *Capital*, 887.

27 **In case of repeat offenders:** See F. M. Eden, *The State of the Poor* (London: 1797), quoted in Marx, "Bloody Legislation Against the Expropriated from the End of the 15th Century Onward," chap. 28 in *Capital*, 897–98.

29 **Even the famous American New Deal:** Tim Barker, "Cold War Capitalism: The Political Economy of American Military Spending, 1947–1990" (doctoral dissertation, Harvard University, 2022).

30 **subject to "land deals":** Eitan Haddock, "Biofuels Land Grab: Guatemala's Farmers Lose Plots and Prosperity to 'Energy Independence,'" *Scientific American*, January 13, 2012, https://www.scientificamerican.com/article/biofuels-land-grab-guatemala/.

30 **Land acquisition in India:** Vasundhara Jairath, "Farmers' Protests: An Opportune Time to Review Our Development Model and Stop the Land Grab," *The Wire*, December 12, 2020, https://thewire.in/agriculture/farmers-protest-opportune-time-review-development-model-land-grab.

30 **The expropriation of the means of subsistence:** As Marxian philosopher Nancy Fraser puts it in *Cannibal Capitalism: How Our System Is Devouring Democracy, Care, and the Planet—and What We Can Do About It* (London: Verso Books, 2022), "Expropriation is an ongoing, albeit unofficial, mechanism of accumulation, which continues alongside the official mechanism of exploitation—Marx's 'front story' so to speak" (7). For two classics on the constitutive role of expropriation, see Rosa Luxemburg, *The Accumulation of Capital* (New York: Monthly Review Press, 1968) and David Harvey, *The New Imperialism* (Oxford: Oxford University Press, 2003).

31 **"The historical movement which changes":** Marx, "The Secret of Primitive Accumulation," chap. 26 in *Capital*, 876.

32 **Economists Lance Taylor and Özlem Ömer show:** Lance Taylor and Özlem Ömer, *Macroeconomic Inequality from Reagan to Trump: Market Power, Wage Repression, Price Inflation, and Industrial Decline* (New York: Cambridge University Press, 2020).

33 **In 2024, 77 percent of American workers:** Lily O'Neill, "Survey Says: San Antonio's PayrollOrg Reveals Majority of American Workers Live Paycheck to Paycheck," *San Antonio Express-News*, October 2, 2024, https://www.expressnews.com/news/article/paycheck-living-payroll-survey-19810554.php.

33 **one out of three Americans:** Megan Brenan, "Record High in U.S. Put Off Medical Care Due to Cost in 2022," Gallup, January 17, 2023, https://news.gallup.com/poll/468053/record-high-put-off-medical-care-due-cost-2022.aspx. Brenan notes, "38% say they put off treatment, up 12 percentage points from 2021."

33 **too expensive or the wait list for it was excessively long:** "Salute, in Italia il 7,6% della popolazione rinuncia alle cure sanitarie: i motivi," *Corriere della sera*, December 30, 2024, https://www.corriere.it

/economia/consumi/24_dicembre_30/salute-in-italia-il-7-6-della
-popolazione-rinuncia-alle-cure-sanitarie-i-motivi-c9e47a84-99f3
-4c76-b838-5d3d872dcxlk.shtml.

33 **It plagued 20 percent of American families:** *The Annual Report of the Council of Economic Advisers* (Council of Economic Advisors, January 20, 1964), 55–61.

34 **Black American workers:** Ellora Derenoncourt and Claire Montialoux, "Minimum Wages and Racial Inequality," *Quarterly Journal of Economics* 136, no. 1 (February 2021): 169–228, https://doi.org/10.1093/qje/qjaa031.

34 **Black Americans are incarcerated:** Michelle Alexander, *The New Jim Crow: Mass Incarceration in the Age of Colorblindness* (New York: New Press, 2010). For an analysis that situates racialized mass incarceration within a classist society, see John Clegg and Adaner Usmani, "The Economic Origins of Mass Incarceration," *Catalyst* 3, no. 3 (2019): 9–53, https://catalyst-journal.com/2019/12/the-economic-origins-of-mass-incarceration.

34 **victimized by predatory loans:** Janis Sarra and Cheryl L. Wade, *Predatory Lending and the Destruction of the African-American Dream* (Cambridge: Cambridge University Press, 2020).

34 **Class and racial oppression are inextricable:** For a reconstruction of the rich tradition of Black Marxism and its analysis of the complex relationship between class and race, see Robin D. G. Kelley, *Freedom Dreams: The Black Radical Imagination* (Boston: Beacon Press, 2002), chap. 2. For two classic texts, see W. E. B. Du Bois, *Black Reconstruction in America, 1860–1880* (New York: Harcourt, Brace and Company, 1935) and C. L. R. James, *The Black Jacobins: Toussaint L'Ouverture and the San Domingo Revolution*, 2nd ed. (New York: Vintage Books, 2001).

34 **The history of slavery and systemic racism:** For a groundbreaking analysis that theorizes American slavery as a moment of global capitalism and enslaved people as part of the modern working class, see McNally, *Slavery and Capitalism*. Figures on the wealth gap between Black and white Americans come from Ellora Derenoncourt, Chi Hyun Kim, Moritz Kuhn, and Moritz Schularick, "Wealth of Two Nations: The U.S. Racial Wealth Gap, 1860–2020," *The Quarterly Journal of Economics* 139, no. 2 (May 2024): 693–750, https://doi.org/10.1093/qje/qjad044.

35 **The capitalist system's tendency:** Fraser, *Cannibal Capitalism*; Stephen Maher and Scott Aquanno, *The Fall and Rise of American Finance: From J. P. Morgan to BlackRock* (New York: Verso Books, 2024).

35 **The former can delegate their administrators:** Branko Milanović, *Capitalism, Alone: The Future of the System That Rules the World* (Cambridge, MA: Belknap Press of Harvard University Press, 2019).

Milanović observes the evolution of our system toward a reality in which among the economic elite, the proportion of those who have both high capital income and high labor income is increasing. However, this serves to only increase polarization and social disparity. As Milanović explains, "The correspondence between high capital and high labor income fuels disparities but, even more importantly, makes it much more difficult to initiate economic policies aimed at reducing inequality."

36 **how unevenly this wealth:** Indeed, the measure to assess economic progress is usually GDP per capita. This measure just divides the total GDP by the number of inhabitants, without any reference to the actual distribution of resources. For example, in a country of only two people, if the total GDP is $1 million, the per capita income averages out to $500,000. However, the reality could be that one of these two individuals is earning $960,000 while the other is only making $40,000. Hence, the GDP per capita fails to register the stark inequality that exists in this scenario. On the history and criticism of using GDP as a measure, read Lorenzo Fioramonti, *Gross Domestic Problem: The Politics Behind the World's Most Powerful Number* (London: Zed Books, 2013).

36 **environmental toll of producing such wealth:** The metabolic connection between capital accumulation and destruction of nature is a fundamental theme in ecological Marxism that takes inspiration from Marx himself, who stressed how our capitalist relations of production transformed who we are and our relations to nature, both how we conceive of it as a mere instrumental object and how we plunder it. Already in *Capital*, Marx wrote: "Capitalist agriculture is a progress in the art of not only robbing the worker but of robbing the soil; all progress in increasing the fertility of the soil for a given time, is a progress of ruining the more long-lasting sources of that fertility. The more a country proceeds from large scale industry as the background of its development, as in the case of the United States, the more rapid is the process of destruction. Capitalist production, therefore, only develops the techniques and the degree of combination of the social process of production by simultaneously undermining the original sources of all wealth—the soil and the worker." ("Machinery and Modern Industry," chap. 15 in *Capital*, 638). For a classic text on these themes, see John Bellamy Foster, *The Ecological Rift: Capitalism's War on the Earth* (New York: Monthly Review Press, 2010); see also Kohei Saito, *Slow Down: The Degrowth Manifesto* (New York: Astra, 2024); and Fraser, *Cannibal Capitalism*, especially chap. 4.

36 **added $2 trillion to their wealth:** "Billionaire Wealth Surges by $2 Trillion in 2024, Three Times Faster Than the Year Before, While the Number of People Living in Poverty Has Barely Changed Since 1990," press release, Oxfam International, January 20, 2025, https://www.oxfam.org/en/press-releases/billionaire-wealth-surges-2-trillion-2024-three

-times-faster-year-while-number. See also World Bank, *Poverty at-a-Glance*, 2024, https://www.worldbank.org/en/topic/poverty.

38 **No one is cheating anyone:** Many Marxian scholars have stressed that forms of expropriation, robbery, and theft play roles under capitalism that are structural to it and are often connected to forms of racial oppression. For example, David Harvey speaks about "accumulation by dispossession" as a phenomenon that magnified during the neoliberal period and has to do with the various ways capital holders use their position and the mass of wealth under their command to appropriate as much value for themselves as possible, both by legal and illegal means. See David Harvey, *The Story of Capital: What Everyone Should Know About How Capital Works* (New York: Penguin Random House, 2026).

38 **In slave societies:** For an insightful study of the economy of American slavery, see McNally, *Slavery and Capitalism*.

39 **Everything is good and fair:** James Kenneth Galbraith and Jing Chen put it accurately: "In mainstream economics, production theory is built around the concept of a production function. In these functions, and the theory that underlies them, there is no *decision* to produce. The decision is assumed; production always occurs to the maximum feasible extent; resources (including labor) are not left unemployed. At both the micro- and the macroeconomic levels, the production function is a parable of cooperation between capital and labor in the production of goods and services. It also provides the basis of a theory of wages and profits, relating each to the contribution they make to total output. Production functions work to rationalize and to justify market processes and market distributions. They associate the high incomes of some people with their productivity, which is very comforting to those people." James K. Galbraith and Jing Chen, *Entropy Economics: The Living Basis of Value and Production* (Chicago: University of Chicago Press, 2025).

39 **It is one constructed with stubborn precision:** E. K. Hunt and Mark Lautzenheiser, *History of Economic Thought: A Critical Perspective* (Abingdon: Routledge, 2015).

40 **This extra value:** In the Marxian framework, the fundamental distinction between labor and labor power presupposes a further fundamental distinction between concrete and abstract labor. Concrete labor is not something specific to capitalism and it originates use value, which encapsulates our concrete use of the goods we produce. What is key to capital accumulation is actually abstract labor, that is, the homogenous quantification of labor that dismisses the subjective experience of the worker. Abstract labor forms the substance of value that normally takes the monetary form. See Marx, "The Commodity," chap. 1 in *Capital*; and Heinreich, *Value, Labor, Money*, chap. 3.

40 **An Instagram video:** More Perfect Union (@perfectunion) and Jessica (Ka) Burbank (@kaburbank), "Maybe the relationship between the

boss and the workers isn't exactly what you were taught," Instagram, January 22, 2024, https://www.instagram.com/reel/C2alPMDOeS3/.

41 **"The working class doesn't only work in its workplace":** Tithi Bhattacharya, "What Is Social Reproduction Theory?," *Socialist Worker*, September 10, 2013, https://socialistworker.org/2013/09/10/what-is-social-reproduction-theory. For a classic in social reproduction theory, see Lise Vogel, *Marxism and the Oppression of Women: Toward a Unitary Theory* (Leiden: Brill/Haymarket, 2013).

42 **The capitalist system is driven to increase exploitation:** For a thorough explanation of Marxian concepts such as surplus value and the rate of exploitation, see Duncan Foley, *Understanding Capital: Marx's Economic Theory* (Cambridge, MA: Harvard University Press, 1986).

42 **While central planning may prevail within a corporation:** On the topic of planning within companies, refer to the classic work: John Kenneth Galbraith, *The New Industrial State* (Turin: Einaudi, 1968).

43 **Thus, Netflix replaced Blockbuster:** Thier, *A People's Guide to Capitalism*, 114.

43 **the rate of exploitation of workers to produce the iPhone X:** *The Rate of Exploitation (The Case of the iPhone)*, Notebook No. 2 (Tricontinental: Institute for Social Research, 2019), https://thetricontinental.org/the-rate-of-exploitation-the-case-of-the-iphone/. In their calculations the authors acknowledge Apple's pricing power but this does not alter their results.

44 **During the nineteenth century and much of the twentieth:** Clara E. Mattei, *The Capital Order: How Economists Invented Austerity and Paved the Way to Fascism* (Chicago: University of Chicago Press, 2022), particularly chap. 3.

44 **surplus value generated by workers:** The classics from Smith to Ricardo to Marx hypothesized that wages could not fall below a limit beyond which the working class risked not reproducing itself.

45 **key to the economic miracle in Western countries:** For trends in real wages and productivity, refer to the graph in Anwar Shaikh, *Capitalism: Competition, Conflict, Crises* (New York: Oxford University Press, 2016), 730–31.

45 **more than 44 percent of American full-time workers:** Emma Burleigh, "More Than 40% of Full-Time U.S. Employees Aren't Making a Living Wage," *Fortune*, August 26, 2024, https://fortune.com/2024/08/26/many-us-workers-dont-make-living-wage-women-people-of-color/; Kathryn Mayer, "Nearly Half of Full-Time Workers Aren't Making a Living Wage," *SHRM*, September 16, 2024, https://www.shrm.org/topics-tools/news/benefits-compensation/nearly-half-of-full-time-workers-aren-t-making-a-living-wage.

45 **In the United States, McDonald's and Walmart:** Hannah Miao, "Walmart and McDonald's Are Among Top Employers of Medicaid

and Food Stamp Beneficiaries, Report Says," CNBC, November 19, 2020, https://www.cnbc.com/2020/11/19/walmart-and-mcdonalds-among-top-employers-of-medicaid-and-food-stamp-beneficiaries.html.

45 **in 2020, 70 percent of Americans receiving state aid:** US Government Accountability Office, *Low-Income Workers: Millions of Full-Time Workers in the Private Sector Rely on Federal Health Care and Food Assistance Programs*, February 25, 2021, https://www.gao.gov/products/gao-21-410t; see also Economic Policy Institute, *State of Working America*, for various reports on wage trends in the US.

45 **more than half of the homeless population is employed:** Bruce D. Meyer et al., "Learning About Homelessness Using Linked Survey and Administrative Data," Becker Friedman Institute for Economics at the University of Chicago, June 23, 2021, https://bfi.uchicago.edu/wp-content/uploads/2021/06/Learning-About-Homelessnessv2.pdf, 2; Brian Goldstone, *There Is No Place for Us: Working and Homeless in America* (New York: Crown, 2025).

45 **in societies where the economy is increasingly based on the service sector:** For a book that illustrates the impacts of this structural factor of low wages in the US economy on higher education and how the dominant narrative has to hide these underlying realities to push for college applications and increasing student indebtedness, see Neil Kraus, *The Fantasy Economy: Neoliberalism, Inequality, and the Education Reform Movement* (Cham: Springer, 2021).

46 **"I'm a human being, not a robot":** Michael Sainato, "'I'm Not a Robot': Amazon Workers Condemn Unsafe, Grueling Conditions at Warehouse," *The Guardian*, February 5, 2020, https://www.theguardian.com/technology/2020/feb/05/amazon-workers-protest-unsafe-grueling-conditions-warehouse.

46 **excessive psycho-physical stress:** See the excellent documentary *Amazon Empire: The Rise and Reign of Jeff Bezos*, directed by James Jacoby, *Frontline*, PBS, February 18, 2020, https://www.pbs.org/wgbh/frontline/documentary/amazon-empire/.

46 **"Workers forced to work for these algorithms":** Yanis Varoufakis, *Technofeudalism: What Killed Capitalism* (London: Penguin Books, 2023), 85.

47 **The extent to which the economic success:** According to a report in *The Hill*, Amazon spent close to $14 million in 2022 on labor consultants. See Karl Evers-Hillstrom, "Amazon Spent Unmatched $14 Million on Labor Consultants in Anti-Union Push," *The Hill*, April 3, 2023, https://thehill.com/business/3931442-amazon-spent-unmatched-14-million-on-labor-consultants-in-anti-union-push/.

47 **three workplace deaths per day in 2024:** "Work-Related Accidents Down but More Deaths in 2024 - INAIL," ANSA English, February 4, 2025, https://www.ansa.it/english/news/general_news/2025/02/04

/work-related-accidents-down-but-more-deaths-in-2024-inail_557dfeda-12d8-4dfb-a85e-536157fa06ed.html.

47 **So long as other workers are available:** Certainly the interest of individual capitalists to reduce production costs may trump the interest of the whole capitalist class that presupposes maintaining a workforce that is alive and productive. This, as Marxian scholars know, is a typical contradiction of our economic system, which was often mitigated historically, with the state stepping in to supporting labor protection laws and thus capital accumulation more generally.

47 **"cannot exist without constantly revolutionising":** Karl Marx and Friedrich Engels, *The Communist Manifesto*, introduction by David Harvey (London: Pluto, 2008), 38.

49 **In the following decade, the number of stores opened increased:** Thier, *A People's Guide to Capitalism*, 119.

49 **chain of 10,623 locations worldwide:** Thomas Ozbun, "Walmart: Number of Stores Globally FY2008–FY2023," Statista, May 22, 2024, https://www.statista.com/statistics/256172/total-number-of-walmart-stores-worldwide/.

49 **Walmart workers earn about 14.5 percent less:** *Wal-Mart: The High Cost of Low Price*, directed by Robert Greenwald (2005), Top Documentary Films, https://topdocumentaryfilms.com/wal-mart-the-high-cost-of-low-price/.

49 **highest number of workers who are beneficiaries of public food subsidies:** US Government Accountability Office, *Federal Social Safety Net Programs: Millions of Full-Time Workers Rely on Federal Health Care and Food Assistance Programs*, GAO-21-45, November 18, 2020, https://www.gao.gov/products/gao-21-45.

49 **"when Wal-Mart entered a county":** Arindrajit Dube, T. William Lester, and Barry Eidlin, "A Downward Push: The Impact of Wal-Mart Stores on Retail Wages and Benefits," UC Berkeley Labor Center, 2007, https://laborcenter.berkeley.edu/a-downward-push-the-impact-of-wal-mart-stores-on-retail-wages-and-benefits/.

49 **Google has transformed:** Shoshana Zuboff, *The Age of Surveillance Capitalism* (Rome: Luiss University Press, 2019).

50 **Workers' exploitation generates:** There is no direct correspondence between the profit of an individual capitalist and the exploitation of their workers. This is because the labor of each worker contributes to a quantity of surplus value that is then divided among different types of capitalists: bankers, landowners, merchants, and so on. Capital investment in circulation, distribution, and realization cannot produce value, but such investments do create the "conditions of possibility" for the realization and appropriation of value and surplus value in the industrial circuit. For further insights on this topic, refer to Foley, *Understanding Capital*, 105–25.

50 **The dominance of one faction:** Extensive literature exists on the rise of finance in the so-called neoliberal era and its role in shaping the latest stages of contemporary capitalism; see Cedric Durand, *Fictitious Capital: How Finance Is Appropriating Our Future* (London: Verso Books, 2017); and Costas Lapavitsas, *Theorizing Financialization* (London: Routledge, 2011). The most common take, even among the Marxian literature, is one that opposes finance to the real industrial economy as corrosive and parasitic to it. This is true especially of much of the progressive literature that, since Keynes, opposes the "good" manufacturing capitalism to "bad" finance capital, attributing a whole series of socioeconomic issues, especially the excessive rise of inequality and instability, to this "cancer of the real economy." Scott Aquanno and Stephen Maher's *The Fall and Rise of American Finance: From J. P. Morgan to BlackRock* (New York: Verso Books, 2022) brilliantly challenges existing accounts by exploring the deep interdependence of finance capital and industrial capital since the early days of capitalism:

> All capitalists are in essence financiers, faced with the choice of investing in one thing or another and pursuing the most profitable opportunities. Nonetheless, capital is divided into fractions: Finance plays a specific role in the overall structure of accumulation, competitively circulating investment across the various branches of production. Finance depends on industrial profits to receive interest, while industry engages with the financial system to raise investment and circulate capital. (19)

In this compelling reading, greater financialization only boosts the exploitative tendencies of capitalism as a socioeconomic system; it has enhanced competitive discipline on industrial firms and has provided managers with the tools to pursue new profit maximizing strategies.

51 **the pressure to stay in business:** For an entertaining and insightful book on the rise of cloud capital and its implications for industrial capital and especially for common people, who often operate as "cloud serfs" in working for free and voluntarily to add content to digital platforms such as YouTube, Instagram, and TikTok, see Varoufakis, *Technofeudalism*. Even if the author claims that it is at the basis of a different system, we can definitely understand these dynamics as an evolved form of capitalism in which appropriation of surplus through rent predominates.

51 **The new frontier of centralization:** An analysis of the success of asset managers and their recent interest in green infrastructure is contained in Brett Christophers, *Our Lives in Their Portfolios: Why Asset Managers Own the World* (New York: Verso Books, 2023).

52 **BlackRock, Vanguard, and State Street, displaced the banks:** Maher and Aquanno, *The Fall and Rise of American Finance*; see especially chap. 5, 146–94.

52 **Attempts to alleviate the burden of real competition:** Mainstream literature takes for granted the "quantity theory of competition,"

according to which competitiveness is a function of the number of competing firms in each sector. Our critical lens instead stresses that, as long as capital is free to move at a global scale both among sectors and between sectors, real competition remains the disciplinary dynamic that binds all capitalists. Indeed, capital flows into those spheres yielding the highest returns and away from those producing the lowest returns. For a technical and detailed discussion on these issues, see Shaikh, *Capitalism*. Aquanno and Maher, in *The Fall and Rise of American Finance*, demonstrate how this theory of competition elucidates the role of financialization and the dominance of major asset managers. Their analysis reveals that rather than hindering real competition, these factors actually enhance it by increasing capital mobility.

54 **"warlike competition reduced to a fairy ballet":** Shaikh, *Capitalism*, 344.

54 **"All the basic tropes of orthodox economics":** Anwar Shaikh, "Anwar Shaikh on Capitalism," interview by Ragupathy Venkatachalam, Goldsmiths, University of London, May 1, 2019, https://economicsppf.com/anwar-shaikh.html. Shaikh, in his real economic analysis approach, offers the most comprehensive contemporary analysis of the phenomenon of real competition.

54 **perfect competition also compromises:** A vast literature stresses the unrealism of the dominant frameworks of competition. This quote of Shaikh's from *Capitalism* is worth reading in full: "Neoclassical writers portray the development of perfect competition and general equilibrium as a movement toward greater analytical precision and rigor in which mathematics plays a decisive role (Stigler 1957, 5). But the capitalism they end up depicting is a parody, purged of all that is dark and destructive, its warlike competition reduced to a fairy ballet. Mathematics is not the problem here, but rather the use to which it is put. How can it be analytically 'rigorous' to reduce human behavior to simple-minded utility-maximizing, business behavior to passive profit-maximizing, and the disaster-punctuated turbulence of competition to a blissful state of rest?" (344). Reference made to George J. Stigler, "Perfect Competition, Historically Contemplated," *Journal of Political Economy* 65, no. 1 (February 1957): 1–17, https://www.jstor.org/stable/1824830.

Chapter 2: The Logic of Austerity

57 **Much economic research has established:** Scholarly research on the economic shortcomings of austerity is vast, especially among the Keynesian literature. For a popularization of these ideas, see Mark Blyth, *Austerity: The History of a Dangerous Idea* (New York: Oxford University Press, 2013).

58 **multinational companies involved in the genocide in Gaza:** Linda J. Bilmes, William D. Hartung, and Stephen Semler, "Costs of War

Report: United States Spending on Israel's Military Operations and Related U.S. Operations in the Region, October 7, 2023–September 30, 2024," Watson Institute for International Public Affairs, October 7, 2024, https://watson.brown.edu/costsofwar/papers/2024/USspending Israel.

58 **In 2022, the official rate of child poverty:** Emily A. Shrider and John Creamer, US Census Bureau, *Poverty in the United States*, 2022 Current Population Reports, P60–280 (Washington, DC: Government Printing Office, September 2023), https://www.census.gov/content/dam/Census/library/publications/2023/demo/p60-280.pdf.

59 **The American state bought nearly $50 billion in arms:** Einar H. Dyvik, "Net Sales of Defense Technology Supplier Lockheed Martin to the U.S. Government from 2000 to 2023," Statista, July 5, 2024, https://www.statista.com/statistics/260877/net-sales-of-lockheed-martin-to-the-us-government/#statisticContainer.

60 **Today, most governments enact regressive tax reforms:** For an astonishing analysis of the regressive tax system in the US and the slew of loopholes that make it even more regressive, see Morris Pearl and Erica Payne, *Tax the Rich! How Lies, Loopholes, and Lobbyists Make the Rich Even Richer* (New York: The New Press, 2021), particularly chap. 3–5.

60 **custodian would have to work two thousand years:** *The American Dream and Other Fairytales*, directed by Abigail Disney and Kathleen Hughes (Chicago Media Project and Fork Films, 2022).

61 **thanks to the mechanism of an annuity trust:** Pearl and Payne, *Tax the Rich!*, 90–94.

61 **AT&T gained a tax windfall of $21 billion:** Michael Sainato, "Bosses Pocket Trump Tax Windfall as Workers See Job Promises Vanish," *The Guardian*, June 16, 2019. For a detailed study on the relation between major tax cuts on the rich and inequality, see David Hope and Julian Limberg, "The Economic Consequences of Major Tax Cuts for the Rich," *Socio-Economic Review* 20, no. 2 (April 2022): 539–59.

62 **Monetary austerity determined the US Federal Reserve's agenda:** "Job Openings and Labor Turnover—July 2024," Bureau of Labor Statistics, press release, August 2024, https://www.bls.gov/news.release/archives/jolts_09042024.htm.

62 **This did not enrich workers:** For greater detail on the relationship between a low interest rate and the concentration of economic power, see Scott Aquanno and Stephen Maher, *The Fall and Rise of American Finance: From J. P. Morgan to BlackRock* (New York: Verso Books, 2024); and Yanis Varoufakis, *Technofeudalism: What Killed Capitalism* (London: Penguin Books, 2024).

64 **taxing capital gains at death:** Pearl and Payne, *Tax the Rich!*, 87.

64 **In 2023 the federal government spent less:** Chris Edwards, "SNAP Spending Doubles to $127 Billion," Cato Institute, April 2, 2023, https://www.cato.org/blog/snap-spending-doubles-127-billion.

64 **The firing of public employees under the pretext:** See Pearl and Payne, *Tax the Rich!*, 87. In fiscal year 2023, the federal government spent $6.13 trillion and collected $4.44 trillion in revenue, resulting in a deficit. The amount by which spending exceeds revenue, $1.69 trillion in 2023, is referred to as deficit spending.

64 **Trump's "One Big Beautiful Bill":** Allie Kelly, "The 'Big Beautiful Bill' Slashes Food Stamps. One Map Shows How Much Red States Depend on Them," *Business Insider*, July 8, 2025, https://www.business insider.com/snap-food-stamp-cuts-republican-could-hurt-red-states-most-2025-5; "Trump's Big Ugly Law Triggers $536 Billion in Medicare Cuts," Democratic Caucus of the House Committee on the Budget, August 15, 2025, https://democrats-budget.house.gov/resources/fact-sheet/trumps-big-ugly-law-triggers-536-billion-medicare-cuts; "CBO Confirms Big Ugly Law Adds 3.4 Trillion to the Deficit, Kicks Millions Off Health Care," Democratic Caucus of the House Committee on the Budget, July 21, 2025, https://democrats-budget.house.gov/news/press-releases/cbo-confirms-big-ugly-law-adds-34-trillion-deficit-kicks-millions-health-care; "Trump's Big Ugly Law Steals from the Poor to Give to the Ultra-Rich," Democratic Caucus of the House Committee on the Budget, August 11, 2025, https://democrats-budget.house.gov/resources/fact-sheet/trumps-big-ugly-law-steals-poor-give-ultra-rich. The latter document also tells us that "families already struggling to make ends meet lose the most. Households in the lowest income decile, making $24,000 a year or less, lose about $1,200 every year, mostly due to deep cuts to Medicaid and food assistance. That amounts to over 3 percent of their total income, a devastating hit for people who can afford it the least."

66 **Investigating what happened a century ago:** The extensive version of this historical analysis can be found in my previous book, Clara E. Mattei, *The Capital Order: How Economists Invented Austerity and Paved the Way to Fascism* (Chicago: University of Chicago Press, 2022).

67 **"If shipping failed":** His Majesty's Stationery Office, *War Cabinet Report 1917*, Cmd. 9005 (London: House of Commons Parliamentary Papers online, 1918), 106, quoted in Mattei, *The Capital Order*.

68 **"on the edge of the abyss":** Leo George Chiozza Money, *The Triumph of Nationalization* (London: Cassell, 1920), 44, viii, https://babel.hathitrust.org/cgi/pt?id=aeu.ark:/13960/t00z8dx5z&view=1up&seq=1.

68 **"National organization and centralized control":** Edward M. H. Lloyd, *Experiments in State Control at the War Office and the Ministry of Food* (London: Clarendon Press, 1924), 23.

68 **"The State, as a war entrepreneur":** Riccardo Bachi, *L'Italia economica nel 1915: annuario della vita commerciale, industriale, agraria, bancaria, finanziaria e della politica economica* (Città di Castello: S. Lapi, 1916), viii.

69 **Indeed, workers were officially equated with soldiers:** Luigi Einaudi, *La condotta economica e gli effetti sociali della guerra italiana* (New Haven, CT: Yale University Press, 1933), 111.

69 **By the end of the war:** Giovanni Procacci, *Dalla rassegnazione alla rivolta: Mentalità e comportamenti popolari nella grande guerra* (Rome: Bulzoni, 1999); Giovanni Procacci, ed., *Stato e classe operaia in Italia durante la prima guerra mondiale* (Milan: FrancoAngeli, 1983).

71 **"The fall of the Hohenzollern in Germany":** Pietro Nenni, *Storia di quattro anni: 1919–1922*, 2nd ed. (Turin: G. Einaudi, 1946), 6.

72 **"material and moral values":** Michele Pietravalle, "Per un ministero della sanità ed assistenza pubblica in Italia," *Nuova antologia* 54, no. 1131 (March 1919): 103–17, see 103–6.

72 **"removed the word 'impossible'":** Jason (pseudonym for J. H. Hammond), *Past and Future* (London: Chatto and Windus, 1918).

72 **"You must be prepared to spend money":** P. K. Clyne, "Reopening the Case of the Lloyd George Coalition and the Post-War Economic Transition," *Journal of British Studies* 10, no. 1 (1970): 162–75, particularly 169.

72 **"It would be no defense":** Christopher Addison, *The Betrayal of the Slums* (London: H. Jenkins, 1922), 5.

73 **It created gardens, playgrounds:** Ministry of Reconstruction Advisory Council, *Women's Housing Sub-Committee Final Report*, Cd. 9232 (London: HMSO, 1919), 20.

73 **"Houses in which mothers could":** Ministry of Reconstruction Advisory Council, *Women's Housing Sub-Committee Final Report*, 13.

73 **"work without thought":** Ministry of Reconstruction, *Adult Education Committee Final Report*, Cmd. 321 (London: HMSO, 1919), 36–37.

74 **"no longer prepared to acquiesce":** G. D. H. Cole, *Chaos and Order in Industry* (London: Methuen, 1920), appendix 1, 250.

74 **These workers occupied land:** The peasants were also granted recognition in the form of an elected representative—*a fiduciario*—to oversee the correct application of the new labor agreement and to form a council of fiduciaries.

74 **Giovanni Giolitti had to admit:** For details, see Mattei, *The Capital Order*, 120–21.

75 **the directors of the main banks:** Angelo Tasca, *Nascita e avvento del fascismo* (Bari: Laterza, 1965).

76 **"announce frequent referenda in their departments":** "Il programma dei commissari di reparto," *L'Ordine nuovo* 1, no. 25 (November 8, 1919): 194.

76 **"absolutely original institutions":** Antonio Gramsci, "Il problema della Commissioni interne," *L'Ordine nuovo*, 1, no. 15 (August 23, 1919): 117–18.

76 **The democratic organization of economic decision-making:** For details on the structure of the councils, see Mattei, *The Capital Order*, 100–116.

NOTES

77 **Monetary and industrial austerity followed:** For details about the policies, see Mattei, *The Capital Order*, chap. 7, 225–45.
78 **"labour and suffering":** League of Nations, *Proceedings of the Brussels International Finance Conference 1920*, vol. 2, *Verbatim Record of the Debate* (London: Harrison and Sons, 1920–1921), 20. For details on the conference and their austerity agenda, see Mattei, *The Capital Order*, 133–60.
79 **"Thanks to Bolshevism":** Maffeo Pantaleoni, *Bolcevismo Italiano* (Bari: G. Laterza, 1922), xiv.
80 **"When the worst happened":** Roberto Marchionatti, ed., *From Our Italian Correspondent: Luigi Einaudi's Articles in "The Economist," 1908–1946* (Florence: L. S. Olschki, 2000), 191–92.
80 **"set of politicians":** Marchionatti, *From Our Italian Correspondent*, 267.
80 **"The important question is":** Marchionatti, *From Our Italian Correspondent*, 263–64.
81 **"We ardently desire a party":** Luigi Einaudi, *Cronache economiche e politiche di un trentennio (1893–1925)*, vol. 5 (Turin: Einaudi, 1963), 921.
81 **"When my young and bold comrades":** Alberto De Stefani, "Il programma finanziario del partito Nazional-Fascista: Lettera aperta al Senatore Luigi Einaudi," *Il popolo d'Italia*, January 14, 1922.
82 **"an Archangel with a flaming sword":** Umberto Ricci, *Tre economisti Italiani: Pantaleoni, Pareto, Loria* (Bari: Laterza, 1939), 44.
83 **"The socialist and the protectionist":** Umberto Ricci, *Dal protezionismo al sindacalismo* (Bari: Laterza, 1926), 25.
83 **"I was seduced by those analyses":** Alberto De' Stefani, "Vilfredo Pareto," *Gerarchia* (1923): 1187–89, 1187.
84 **Ricci believed theoretical constructions:** Umberto Ricci, "Rassegna del movimento scientifico: Economia," *Giornale degli economisti* 36 (May 1908, series 2): 385–405, 389. Note that "tame men" translates from "ammaestrare gli uomini" (my italics).
85 **"does not always appear beautiful":** Ricci, *Dal protezionismo al sindacalismo*, 72.
85 **"By proclaiming the principle":** Ricci, *Dal protezionismo al sindacalismo*, 102.
85 **"This is the celebrated and vulgar":** *Corriere della sera*, April 27, 1920, in Einaudi, *Cronache economiche e politiche di un trentennio*, 720. Note: "Savers are necessary for production?" comes from "I risparmiatori sono necessari alla produzione?"
85 **"a result of savings and conservation":** Alberto De' Stefani, *Lezioni di economia politica: Appunti; anno accademico 1919–20* (Padua: La Litotipo, 1919), 164.
86 **The theoretical assumption is:** According to neoclassical theory, the subjective discount rate expresses the individual evaluation of the utility derived from future consumption compared to current consumption. It thus depends on the patience of the decision-maker: the

more "impatient" the agent is to consume, the lower the evaluation of the well-being derived from future consumption, and the higher their discount rate.

86 **"Amongst the tools with which man can elevate himself"**: Umberto Ricci, *Saggi sul Risparmio* (Lanciano: Carabba, 1999), 7.

86 **"[They] realise almost perfectly"**: Maffeo Pantaleoni, *Pure Economics* (London: Macmillan, 1898), 259.

87 **"the direction of the labour"**: Maffeo Pantaleoni, *Bolcevismo Italiano* (Bari: G. Laterza, 1922), 47–48.

87 **"The classes with lower incomes"**: Pantaleoni, *Bolcevismo Italiano*, 36

88 **"If the newspapers preached abstinence"**: Luigi Einaudi, *Prediche*, 174.

88 **"face the market"**: Alberto F. Alesina, Stephan Danninger, and Massimo Rostagno, "Redistribution Through Public Employment: The Case of Italy," Working Paper No. 7387 (National Bureau of Economic Research, October 1999), https://www.nber.org/system/files/working_papers/w7387/w7387.pdf.

89 **"the wage demanded by unions"**: Alberto Alesina and Silvia Ardagna, "Large Changes in Fiscal Policy: Taxes Versus Spending," *Tax Policy and the Economy* 24 (2010): 35–68, 38.

89 **"For the good of all"**: Veronique de Rugy and Alberto Alesina, "Austerity: The Relative Effects of Tax Increases Versus Spending Cuts" (Mercatus Center at George Mason University, March 7, 2013), https://www.mercatus.org/research/research-papers/austerity-relative-effects-tax-increases-versus-spending-cuts.

89 **"If the French think"**: Alberto Alesina, "The Kindest Cuts," *City Journal*, Autumn 2012, https://www.city-journal.org/article/the-kindest-cuts.

90 **consequence of the "success" of previous austerity**: For a classic study of the economic dynamics that led to the rise of Nazi Germany and a detailed analysis of Nazi economic policies, as well as a reflection on how World War II cannot be explained while dismissing the economic dimension, see Adam Tooze, *Wages of Destruction* (New York: Penguin Books, 2006).

91 **In Pennsylvania, privatized water**: Megan Guy and Dara Donovan, *Measuring Up: Grading Drinking Water Quality, Affordability, and Transparency Practices in Allegheny County Water Systems* (Pittsburgh Water Collaboratory and Women for a Healthy Environment, 2023), https://dscholarship.pitt.edu/45129/4/Water%20Report%20June%202023%20Full.pdf.

91 **"There's class warfare"**: Ben Stein, "In Class Warfare, Guess Which Class Is Winning," *New York Times*, November 26, 2006, https://www.nytimes.com/2006/11/26/business/yourmoney/26every.html.

Chapter 3: The Cruel Math of Unemployment

93 **Dominant economic models:** For an intelligent criticism of neoclassical theory and especially its abstract equilibrium framework, see James K. Galbraith and Jing Chen, *Entropy Economics: The Living Basis of Value and Production* (Chicago: University of Chicago Press, 2025).

93 **efficient enough to guarantee full employment:** Mainstream economics is of course a broad—and in its own way—diverse discipline. The most traditional views argue that, if unhindered by labor regulations, the private economy will come to a full employment equilibrium with competition, in which the marginal disutility of labor is proportional to the money wage, and any remaining unemployment is "frictional," namely expressing the lag due to the processes of people moving from one job to another. This current as typically embodied in the Chicago School of Economics sees no real space for effective macroeconomic intervention, since full employment will be reached automatically by market mechanism. Nowadays most central banks and treasury departments use models that have some Keynesian features, at least in the short run, and thus allow for some flexibility of the fiscal and monetary policy mix to achieve a target rate of unemployment. Nonetheless, this mainstream Keynesianism tends to claim that markets work well to allocate resources (with increasing qualifications concerning inequality) as long as fiscal and monetary policy maintain a politically acceptable level of unemployment. Of course, what is politically acceptable cannot trump the economically acceptable: meaning the employment level cannot be higher than the threshold that can spur inflation.

94 **"Euclidean geometers in a non-Euclidean world":** John Maynard Keynes, *The General Theory of Employment, Interest, and Money* (London: Palgrave Macmillan, 1964), 7.

94 **"The wiles of the prostitute can be far more professional":** John Kenneth Galbraith, *The New Industrial State* (Princeton, NJ: Princeton University Press, 1967), 167.

95 **"It is capitalist accumulation":** Karl Marx, "The General Law of Capitalist Accumulation," chap. 25 in *Capital*, trans. Ben Fowkes, introduction by Ernest Mandel (New York: Penguin Classics, 1992), 783.

96 **agriculture employed about 60 percent of US workers:** Of course, greater capital accumulation means that in absolute terms, more workers can get hired, also in novel sectors that our economy captures, but the overall tendency is for a smaller proportion of labor to be put to work with respect to machines, which highlights an important contradictory tendency of our economy: the expulsion of the source of value (labor) and thus the fall in the profit rate. Clearly, as Marx recognized, in the short run unemployment is the result of the balance of two countervailing outcomes of capitalist accumulation: (a) the displacement of labor through technical change and (b) further capital

accumulation, which instead increases the demand for labor power. Marx himself explains that in the short term, a feedback loop is behind this, since rising unemployment lowers wages and increases profit rates, which accelerates capital accumulation and the demand for labor power. Richard Goodwin formalized this view in his famous model of cyclical accumulation.

96 **We therefore witness a further tendency:** John Maynard Keynes, in his essay "Economic Possibilities for Our Grandchildren," which was the text of a lecture given in Madrid in 1930 and published in *Essays in Persuasion* (London: Macmillan, 1931), demonstrates the utopian optimism that would arise from abandoning the principle of exploitation. He envisions a form of capitalism that evolves spontaneously toward a model in which everyone works very few hours a day, leaving ample leisure time for people to pursue their passions.

98 **When European governments colonized African countries:** Walter Rodney, *How Europe Underdeveloped Africa* (London: Bogle-L'Ouverture, 1972).

99 **youth unemployment reached 42.7 percent:** Regional Agency for Technology, Technology Transfer and Innovation (ARTI), *Tasso di disoccupazione giovanile*, updated on May 21, 2025, accessed June 19, 2025, https://apulianinnovationoverview.arti.puglia.it/indicatori/tasso-di-disoccupazione-giovanile.

99 **According to the 2023 Censis-Eudaimon report:** The report is an annual publication, produced by the Social Investment Study Center (Censis) with Eudaimon (https://eudaimon.it/en/), a benefit corporation in Italy that provides businesses with strategies for better corporate welfare.

99 **employee engagement is low:** Jim Harter and Ryan Pendell, "Global Engagement Falls for the Second Time Since 2009," Gallup, April 23, 2025, https://www.gallup.com/workplace/659279/global-engagement-falls-second-time-2009.aspx.

99 **Almost two-thirds of workers:** Francesca Coin, *Le grandi dimissioni. Il nuovo rifiuto del lavoro e il tempo di riprenderci la vita* (Turin: Einaudi, 2023), 102–7.

99 **"This is hardly a reassuring picture":** Coin, *Le grandi dimissioni*, 106.

100 **"Under a regime of permanent full employment":** Michał Kalecki, "Political Aspects of Full Employment," *Political Quarterly* 14, no. 4 (1943): 322–30. Kalecki explains that full employment could be achievable in an authoritarian capitalist regime, where worker discipline is maintained through explicit oppression by state forces that eliminate unions, the right to strike, and any other form of political dissent.

101 **"The over-work of the employed":** Marx, "The General Law of Capitalist Accumulation," chap. 25 in *Capital*, 790.

NOTES

102 **Especially in times of high social discontent:** Nandita Sharma, *Home Rule: National Sovereignty and the Separation of Natives and Migrants* (New York: Duke University Press, 2020).

102 **"the condition of being defenseless":** Nancy Fraser, *Cannibal Capitalism: How Our System Is Devouring Democracy, Care, and the Planet—and What We Can Do About It* (London: Verso Books, 2022), 40. Fraser stresses how in the division between exploitation and expropriation, capitalism harbors a structural basis for racial oppression. This was true with the confiscation of colonialism and remains true today, globally. See especially chap. 2.

102 **Consider Italy's tomato-sauce export business:** Istituto di Servizi per il Mercato Agricolo Alimentare (Institute of Services for the Agricultural and Food Market), *Focus: Conserve di Pomodoro. Tendenze e dinamiche recenti* (January 2024).

102 **They endure inhumane working conditions:** Mattia Giampaolo and Aurora Ianni, *Il sistema del caporalato in Italia* (Focsiv, 2020), https://www.focsiv.it/wp-content/uploads/2020/12/CSR-n.-1-ITA-14.12.2020.pdf.

102 **vast infrastructure for the 2022 FIFA World Cup:** Pete Pattisson, "Revealed: Qatar's World Cup 'Slaves,'" *The Guardian*, September 25, 2013, https://www.theguardian.com/world/2013/sep/25/revealed-qatars-world-cup-slaves.

103 **two amputations a week across US meat plants:** Matt Reynolds, "US Meat, Milk Prices Should Spike if Donald Trump Carries Out Mass Deportation Schemes," *Wired*, December 11, 2024, https://www.wired.com/story/us-meat-milk-prices-should-spike-if-donald-trump-carries-out-mass-deportation-schemes/.

103 **dropping to 3.4 percent in January 2023:** Bureau of Labor Statistics, *The Employment Situation—January 2023* (US Department of Labor, February 3, 2023), https://www.bls.gov/news.release/archives/empsit_02032023.pdf.

103 **The Bureau of Labor Statistics considers:** Bureau of Labor Statistics, "Labor Force Statistics from the Current Population Survey: How the Government Measures Unemployment," US Department of Labor, https://www.bls.gov/cps/cps_htgm.htm.

103 **maybe double:** This disconnect between the standard unemployment count and the actual reality is also captured by the Bureau of Labor Statistics in the measure called "U-6: Total unemployed, plus all persons marginally attached to the labor force, plus total employed part time for economic reasons, as a percent of the civilian labor force plus all persons marginally attached to the labor force," which is historically nearly double in time with respect to the official rate. For example, in July 2024 it was 8.2 percent with respect to the official rate of 4.5 percent. See table A-15, "Alternative measures of labor underutilization," in Bureau of Labor Statistics, *The Employment Situation—*

NOTES

July 2024 (US Department of Labor, August 2, 2024), https://www.bls.gov/news.release/archives/empsit_08022024.pdf.

103 **"tight to an unhealthy level":** Kai Ryssdal, "Fed Chair Jerome Powell: 'Whether We Can Execute a Soft Landing or Not, It May Actually Depend on Factors That We Don't Control,'" *Marketplace*, May 12, 2022, https://www.marketplace.org/2022/05/12/fed-chair-jerome-powell-controlling-inflation-will-include-some-pain/.

105 **In 2022, the number of strikes rose by 52 percent:** For precise data on strikes and labor actions, refer to the Labor Action Tracker provided by Cornell University, https://www.ilr.cornell.edu/faculty-and-research/labor-action-tracker. This tool is designed to track and analyze strike activities across the United States, offering detailed information about the nature of these strikes, their locations, the industries involved, and the number of participants. It's a valuable resource for anyone looking to understand the current trends and impacts of labor movements in real time.

105 **For instance, Hollywood writers went on strike:** Alissa Wilkinson and Emily Stewart, "The End of the Writers' Strike Is Very, Very Close," *Vox*, September 28, 2023, https://www.vox.com/culture/2023/9/24/23888673/wga-strike-end-sag-aftra-contract.

105 **"The union went on strike despite":** Chris Isidore and Vanessa Yurkevich, "UAW Workers Launch Unprecedented Strike Against All Big Three Automakers," CNN, September 15, 2023, https://www.cnn.com/2023/09/15/business/auto-workers-strike/index.html.

105 **NPR warned that:** Camila Domonoske, "The UAW Won Big in the Auto Strike—but What Does It Mean for the Rest of Us?," NPR, November 12, 2023, https://www.npr.org/2023/11/12/1211602392/uaw-auto-strike-deals-ratified-big-three-shawn-fain; also on the repercussions of the UAW's strike win, see Noah Weiland, "U.A.W. Strike Gains Could Reverberate Far Beyond Autos," *New York Times*, October 31, 2023, https://www.nytimes.com/2023/10/31/business/economy/uaw-labor.html?smid=url-share.

106 **Over time, the curve:** On the theoretical basis and history of the Phillips curve, see Anwar Shaikh, *Capitalism: Competition, Conflict, Crises* (New York: Oxford University Press, 2016), 563–66. As Shaikh and others note, especially after 1973, the Phillips curve had a poor empirical application. However, the Phillips curve remains one of the tools in the Fed's arsenal to predict inflation. For a critique of the Phillips curve, see also James K. Galbraith, "Time to Ditch the NAIRU," *Journal of Economic Perspectives* 11, no. 1 (1997): 93–108.

109 **critical economist Richard D. Wolff emphasizes:** Richard D. Wolff, *Understanding Capitalism* (Chicago: Haymarket Books, 2024).

109 **"sufficient to account for what we observe in meatpacking":** Chuck Abbott, "Packers: We're Not to Blame for High Meat Prices," Agricul-

ture.com, April 28, 2022, https://www.agriculture.com/news/business/packers-we-re-not-to-blame-for-high-meat-prices.

110 **According to these empirical studies:** See, for example, Isabella M. Weber and Evan Wasner, "Sellers' Inflation, Profits and Conflict: Why Can Large Firms Hike Prices in an Emergency?," *Review of Keynesian Economics* 11, no. 2 (April 14, 2023): 183; and Josh Bivens, "Corporate Profits Have Contributed Disproportionately to Inflation. How Should Policymakers Respond?," *Working Economics Blog*, Economic Policy Institute, April 21, 2022. For a contribution that discusses further explanations for inflation, see Marc Lavoie, "Some Controversies in the Causes of the Post-Pandemic Inflation," *Monetary Policy Institute Blog*, Medium, May 14, 2023, https://medium.com/@monetarypolicyinstitute/some-controversies-in-the-causes-of-the-post-pandemic-inflation-1480a7a08eb7.

110 **According to Reich:** See, for example, his article "Corporate Greed, Not Wages, Is Behind Inflation. It's Time for Price Controls," *The Guardian* (US edition), September 25, 2022.

111 **The state, in fact, never loses:** When I talk about the state, I don't mean just the executive branch—namely the government in power and its ministers—but also the legislative organs (parliament), the judiciary, law enforcement bodies, and especially the public institutions involved in economic management, such as the treasury and central banks, composed of economic experts who maintain a good deal of autonomy from the electoral process and are rarely discussed.

111 **"There is no magic tool":** Olivier Blanchard, Adam Domash, and Lawrence H. Summers, "Bad News for the Fed from the Beveridge Space," Peterson Institute for International Economics, Policy Brief 22-7, July 2022, 2.

111 **In July 2024, high interest rates:** James K. Galbraith, "High Interest Rates Finally Bite," *Project Syndicate*, August 6, 2024.

111 **many critical economists dispute:** See for example, James K. Galbraith, "Inflation Shamanism," *Project Syndicate*, September 20, 2024, https://www.project-syndicate.org/commentary/federal-reserve-interest-rate-hikes-did-not-control-inflation-by-james-k-galbraith-2024-09.

Chapter 4: The West over the Rest

114 **The narrow focus on individuals:** For a good criticism of randomized control trials as the main method of mainstream development economics, see Sanjay G. Reddy, "Randomise This! On Poor Economics," *Review of Agrarian Studies* 2, no. 2 (2012): 60–73.

115 **"such as corruption or 'crony capitalism'":** James K. Galbraith and Jing Chen, *Entropy Economics: The Living Basis of Value and Production* (Chicago: University of Chicago Press, 2025), 2.

115 **Global North countries control 69 percent of global wealth:** "Billionaire Wealth Surges by $2 Trillion in 2024, Three Times Faster Than the Year Before, While the Number of People Living in Poverty Has Barely Changed Since 1990," Oxfam International, press release, January 20, 2025, https://www.oxfam.org/en/press-releases/billionaire-wealth-surges-2-trillion-2024-three-times-faster-year-while-number.

115 **As critical scholars Andre Gunder Frank and Samir Amin argue:** Relevant works include Andre Gunder Frank, *Capitalism and Underdevelopment in Latin America: Historical Studies of Chile and Brazil* (New York: Monthly Review Press, 1967); Andre Gunder Frank, *Dependent Accumulation and Underdevelopment* (New York: Monthly Review Press, 1979); Samir Amin, *Accumulation on a World Scale: A Critique of the Theory of Underdevelopment* (New York: Monthly Review Press, 1974); Samir Amin, *Imperialism and Unequal Development* (New York: Monthly Review Press, 1977); Samir Amin, *Eurocentrism*, 2nd ed. (New York: Monthly Review Press, 2010).

117 **Critical economists have captured the dynamics:** The literature in critical developmental economics that is sensitive to the crucial historical link with colonialism and imperialism and builds on the concept of dependency is diverse and evolving. Classics include Paul A. Baran, *Political Economy of Growth* (New York: Monthly Review Press, 1957); Raúl Prebisch, *The Economic Development of Latin America and Its Principal Problems* (New York: United Nations, 1962); Theotonio dos Santos, "The Structure of Dependence," *American Economic Review* 60, no. 2 (1970): 231–36; Arghiri Emmanuel, *Unequal Exchange: A Study of the Imperialism of Trade* (New York: Monthly Review Press, 1972); and Samir Amin, *Accumulation on a World Scale* (New York: Monthly Review Press, 1974). For more recent literature, see also Ruy Mauro Marini, "The Dialectics of Dependence: An Approach to the Theory of Dependency," *Latin American Perspectives* 1, no. 2 (1974): 3–21; Fathimah Musthaq, "Dependency in a Financialised Global Economy," *Review of African Political Economy* 48, no. 167 (2021): 15–31; Ingrid Harvold Kvangraven, "Beyond the Stereotype: Restating the Relevance of the Dependency Research Programme," *Development and Change* 52, no. 1 (2021): 76–112.

117 **In June 2024, Ghana took out its eighteenth IMF loan:** For details on the case of Ghana and the politics of monetary austerity, see Jan R. Hendricks, "Monetary Imperialism and the Money Form of Value: The Case of the 2022–23 Ghanaian Sovereign Debt Crisis" (master of philosophy thesis, University of Oxford, 2023).

118 **But in the same year, $203 billion:** Karen McVeigh, "World Is Plundering Africa's Wealth of 'Billions of Dollars a Year,'" *The Guardian*, May 24, 2017.

119 **Oxfam reports that in 2024:** Oxfam America, *Takers, Not Makers: The Unjust Poverty and Unearned Wealth of Colonialism* (Oxfam,

NOTES

2024), 5, https://www.oxfamamerica.org/explore/research-publica tions/takers-not-makers/.

119 **Pressure to attract foreign capital:** Pablo G. Bortz and Annina Kaltenbrunner, "The International Dimension of Financialization in Developing and Emerging Economies," *Development and Change* 49, no. 2 (2018): 375–93.

120 **21 million children deeply malnourished:** "Millions in Southern Africa Facing Worst Food Crisis in Decades, Warns WFP," *Reuters*, October 16, 2024, https://www.reuters.com/world/africa/millions -southern-africa-facing-worst-food-crisis-decades-warns-wfp-2024 -10-15/.

120 **invisible to citizens in the Global North:** Kohei Saito, *Slow Down: The Degrowth Manifesto* (New York: Astra, 2024), 26.

121 **"total control of energy resources":** Quote from Palestinian worker in Francesca Albanese and Christian Elia, *J'Accuse* (Milan: Fuori Scena, 2023), 61–62.

121 **Proof of this is Israel's GDP per person:** A UN report published in 1991 has a large number of tables on national accounts of the West Bank and Gaza Strip from 1968 to 1987. See UN Conference on Trade and Development, *Selected National Accounts Series of the Occupied Palestinian Territory (West Bank and Gaza Strip), 1968–1987*, UNCTAD/RDP/SEU/6, (November 25, 1991), https://unctad.org /system/files/official-document/rdpseud6_en.pdf.

122 **Nearly half of all goods imported from Israel:** Ibrahim Shikaki, "The Political Economy of Dependency and Class Formation in the Occupied Palestinian Territories Since 1967," in *Political Economy of Palestine*, ed. Alaa Tartir, Tariq Dana, and Timothy Seidel (Cham, Switzerland: Palgrave Macmillan, 2021), 56.

122 **granted concessions on natural resources:** Barbara Smith, "Monopoly Rights for Jewish Enterprise," chap. 6 in *The Roots of Separatism in Palestine: British Economic Policy, 1920–1929* (Syracuse University Press, 1993). In particular, see pp. 119 and 130.

123 **During the Nakba:** On the Nakba, see Ilan Pappe, *The Ethnic Cleansing of Palestine* (London: Oneworld, 2006). The number of Arab Palestinians who remained in the newly established state of Israel was less than 20 percent of the population that was living there.

124 **Between 1967 and 1971, the Israeli military:** Jaclynn Ashly, "Investigation: The Palestinian Struggle for Labor Rights in Israel," *Jacobin*, April 2, 2024, https://jacobin.com/2024/04/palestine-labor-unions -occupation-apartheid.

125 **Israel controls the borders:** Shir Hever, in *The Political Economy of Israel's Occupation: Repression Beyond Exploitation* (London: Pluto Press, 2010), an important book to dig deeper into the multiple aspect of dependence, writes, "The loss of revenue to the Palestinian economy during the years from 1970 to 1987 as a result of the one-sided

customs envelope totaled US $6–11 billion, or about 13 percent of the Palestinians' GDP." He explains the political consequence of economic subjugation: "The Palestinian Authority's reliance on income collected on its behalf by Israel has made it very vulnerable to pressure from Israeli economic interests. The Palestinian Authority has failed to improve the living conditions of Palestinians under occupation, and the practicalities of its own survival have often pushed it to act in collusion with Israel's occupation policies" (33–35).

125 **These obstacles create high transportation costs:** On the inflationary effects of the occupation, see Hever, *The Political Economy of Israel's Occupation*, chap. 3, especially 71–76.

125 **It collects import taxes:** The economic protocol stipulates that 3 percent of tax funds be deducted for the benefit of Israel (as an administrative commission). See Mahmoud Abu Ebaya, "Piracy of Clearance Revenues, an Israeli Weapon of Financial Blockade on Palestinians," WAFA, Palestinian News and Info Agency, https://english.wafa.ps/Pages/Details/144991.

126 **In the winter of 2015:** "Israel and Palestinians 'Reach Accord' on Frozen Taxes," Al Jazeera, April 18, 2015, https://www.aljazeera.com/news/2015/4/18/israel-and-palestinians-reach-accord-on-frozen-taxes.

126 **The Palestinian Authority cannot provide:** International Labour Organization, *Impact of the COVID-19 Pandemic on the Labour Market in the Occupied Palestinian Territory: A Forecasting Model Assessment* (September 2020), 9.

127 **Israeli state-run electricity company in payment for past debts:** Steven Scheer, "Israel to Use Withheld Palestinian Tax Income to Pay Electric Co Debt," Reuters, January 12, 2025, https://www.reuters.com/world/middle-east/israel-use-withheld-palestinian-tax-income-pay-electric-co-debt-2025-01-12/.

127 **Israeli appropriation of water:** For further details on the topic of water colonial apartheid in Palestine, see Clemens Messerschmid, "Hydro-Apartheid and Water Access in Israel-Palestine: Challenging the Myths of Cooperation and Scarcity," in *Decolonizing Palestinian Political Economy*, ed. Mandy Turner and Omar Shweiki (London: Palgrave Macmillan, 2014); and Stephen Gasteyer, Jad Isaac, Jane Hillal, and Sean Walsh, "Water Grabbing in Colonial Perspective: Land and Water in Israel/Palestine," *Water Alternatives* 5 no. 2 (2012): 450–68.

128 **"largely spared any significant water reduction":** Human Rights Council, *The Allocation of Water Resources in the Occupied Palestinian Territory, Including East Jerusalem: Report of the United Nations High Commissioner for Human Rights*, A/HRC/48/43, 9 (October 15, 2021), https://docs.un.org/en/A/HRC/48/43.

128 **"crisis levels":** Quoted in Human Rights Council, *The Allocation of Water Resources*, 11.

NOTES

128 **chronic electricity deficit:** Human Rights Council, *The Allocation of Water Resources*, 13.

128 **This catastrophic man-made drought:** "Water Is Being Used as a Weapon of War in Gaza," Médecins Sans Frontières / Doctors Without Borders, March 25, 2025, https://www.doctorswithoutborders.org/latest/water-being-used-weapon-war-gaza.

129 **However, twenty years later the number of self-employed:** On the question of Palestinian labor and land dispossession, see Lelia Farakesh, *Palestinian Labour Migration to Israel: Labour, Land, and Occupation* (United Kingdom: Taylor and Francis, 2005).

129 **Israeli employers pay Palestinians more:** As local sources of income are constantly suppressed by Israeli authorities, a crucial income to the Palestinians became remittances from Palestinian workers working in Israel, in the Jewish settlements in the occupied Palestinian territories, and in the Gulf states.

130 **"It is almost impossible to fire an Israeli worker":** Quoted in Shikaki, "The Political Economy of Dependency and Class Formation," 52.

130 **The number of non-Palestinian workers in Israel:** Ishac Diwan and Radwan A. Shaban, eds., *Development Under Adversity: The Palestinian Economy in Transition* (Washington, DC: World Bank, 1999).

130 **severe underdevelopment of the Palestinian economy:** On the political economy of international aid and its effect on the Palestinian and Israeli economies, see Hever, *The Political Economy of Israel's Occupation*, chap. 2 and 3. It is interesting to note that aid has helped strengthen Israel's currency, especially since, due to structural inflation in the occupied territories, donors of aid have had to convert massive amounts of foreign currency at Israel's central bank, causing the foreign currency reserves at the Bank of Israel to swell. As Hever writes, "Israel has been able to . . . turn the misery of Palestinians into a source of foreign currency inflow" (49).

131 ***Haaretz* described the wall:** Antony Loewenstein, *The Palestine Laboratory: How Israel Exports the Technology of Occupation Around the World* (London: Verso Books, 2023), 74.

131 **"an open-air prison":** "Gaza: An 'Open-Air Prison,'" Human Rights Watch, June 13, 2022, https://www.hrw.org/video-photos/video/2022/06/13/gaza-open-air-prison.

131 **over seventeen thousand children:** "Gaza War: UN Officials Warn of Unspeakable Conditions as Children Bear the Brunt," UN News, July 16, 2025, https://news.un.org/en/story/2025/07/1165415.

131 **"A whole classroom of children killed":** Sarah Ferguson, "Desperate Situation for Gaza's 1 Million Children," UNICEF USA, July 24, 2025, https://www.unicefusa.org/stories/desperate-situation-gazas-1-million-children.

131 **politically engineered famine:** Malak A. Tantesh and Emma Graham-Harrison, "'We Faced Hunger Before, but Never Like This':

Skeletal Children Fill Hospital Wards as Starvation Grips Gaza," *The Guardian*, July 23, 2025, https://www.theguardian.com/world/2025/jul/23/we-faced-hunger-before-but-never-like-this-skeletal-children-fill-hospital-wards-as-starvation-grips-gaza.

132 **Palestinians have been the most surveilled population:** Loewenstein, *The Palestine Laboratory*, 87.

132 **"It's growing geometrically":** Loewenstein, *The Palestine Laboratory*, 55.

132 **While the European Union uses its Heron drones:** Loewenstein, *The Palestine Laboratory*, see chap. 1 and 2.

133 **"most militarized region in the world":** "From Kashmir to Palestine: Rebellion—the Permanent Revolution!" *New York War Crimes* 2, no. 12, August 18, 2024, https://newyorkwarcrimes.com/print-issue-vol-ii-no-12.

133 **The ground itself is so polluted:** Given the level of destruction to the economic fabric in 2024, GDP per capita levels are estimated to need at least until 2028 to revert to 2022 levels. Even under optimal circumstances of a recovery driven by double-digit growth rates and a substantial foreign aid, welfare levels will take decades to revert to their dire pre-October 2023 benchmark. See UN Conference on Trade and Development, *Preliminary Assessment of the Economic Impact of the Destruction in Gaza and Prospects for Economic Recovery*, UNCTAD/OSG/INF/2024/1, 12 (January 2024), https://unctad.org/system/files/official-document/osginf2024d1_en.pdf.

133 **The few surviving Palestinians:** For an anatomy of the ongoing genocide, see Human Rights Council, *Anatomy of a Genocide: Report of the Special Rapporteur on the Situation of Human Rights in the Palestinian Territories Occupied Since 1967*, Francesca Albanese, A/HRC/55/73, (July 1, 2024), https://documents.un.org/symbol-explorer?s=A/HRC/55/73&i=A/HRC/55/73_1725462735821.

133 **The ongoing genocide:** On articles related to the genocide, see *"You Feel Like You Are Subhuman": Israel's Genocide Against Palestinians in Gaza*, Amnesty International (December 5, 2024), https://www.amnesty.org/en/documents/mde15/8668/2024/en/; and UN General Assembly, *Genocide as Colonial Erasure: Report of the Special Rapporteur on the Situation of Human Rights in the Palestinian Territories Occupied Since 1967*, Francesca Albanese, A/79/384 (October 1, 2024), https://www.un.org/unispal/document/genocide-as-colonial-erasure-report-francesca-albanese-01oct24/.

133 **crime against humanity:** "Israeli Actions in Palestinian Territories Constitute War Crimes, Human Rights Council Hears," UN News, June 17, 2025, https://news.un.org/en/story/2025/06/1164496.

134 **plans for lucrative reconstruction:** Adam Tooze, "Chartbook 284: Gaza: The Decade After," *Chartbook*, May 23, 2024, https://adamtooze.substack.com/p/chartbook-284-gaza-the-decade-after.

NOTES

134 **America's biggest banks are cashing in:** BankTrack, PAX, and Profundo, "Seven Underwriters of 'War Bonds' Instrumental in Enabling Israel's Assault on Gaza, New Research Finds," February 14, 2025, https://www.banktrack.org/news/seven_underwriters_of_war_bonds_instrumental_in_enabling_israel_s_assault_on_gaza_new_research_finds.

135 **one-third of the country's children:** "Israel Report: About Two Million People Live Below the Poverty Line," *Jerusalem Post*, December 16, 2020, https://www.jpost.com/israel-news/israel-report-about-two-million-people-live-below-the-poverty-line-656317.

135 **Because of the increased trade:** For more on this topic, see Jamil Hilal, "Class Transformation in the West Bank and Gaza," *MERIP Reports* 53 (1976): 9–15; and Adel Samara, *The Political Economy of the West Bank 1967–1987: From Peripheralization to Development* (London: Khamsin, 1988).

136 **"It's no wonder that 79 percent":** Ladislau Dowbor, "The Financial Drain in Brazil," August 4, 2023, https://dowbor.org/2023/07/the-financial-drain-in-brazil.html.

136 **30 percent of Brazil's GDP:** Dowbor, "The Financial Drain in Brazil."

137 **one-third of families lack a secure source of food:** Archana Shukla, "Sri Lanka's Children Go Hungry as Food Prices Soar," BBC, December 8, 2022, https://www.bbc.com/news/business-63868497.

138 **In this way our economic system tends to devour:** Nancy Fraser, *Cannibal Capitalism: How Our System Is Devouring Democracy, Care, and the Planet—and What We Can Do About It* (London: Verso Books, 2022).

138 **from 2015 to 2023 the EU spent:** Loewenstein, *The Palestine Laboratory*, chap. 4.

138 **The same corporations that make profits:** Loewenstein, *The Palestine Laboratory*, 101.

138 **including at least 1,328 children:** "Missing Migrants: Mediterranean," International Organization for Migration (IOM), accessed August 18, 2024, https://missingmigrants.iom.int/region/mediterranean.

138 **paying millions to at least thirteen military companies:** Loewenstein, *The Palestine Laboratory*, 132–33.

Chapter 5: Democracy Is Anti-Capitalism

139 **"Fascism has surely brought order out of chaos":** Letter to John Pierpont "Jac" Morgan Jr., November 19, 1926, box 307, folder 27, Governor's Files, Bank of England Archive. Also reprinted in Clara E. Mattei, *The Capital Order: How Economists Invented Austerity and Paved the Way to Fascism* (Chicago: University of Chicago Press, 2022), 257.

139 **provided vital financial support to Mussolini's dictatorship:** For an in-depth study of the House of Morgan's support for the fascist regime,

and the compliance of the broader American financial establishment, see Gian Giacomo Migone, *The United States and Fascist Italy: The Rise of American Finance in Europe*, trans. Molly Tambor (Cambridge University Press, 2015).

140 ***The Times* enthusiastically welcomed:** "Fascismo," *The Times*, July 2, 1923, 13.

140 **It is common among well-meaning liberals:** For details on the Italian and British case after World War I, see Mattei, *The Capital Order*, chap. 6–9.

142 **"Chile without an authoritarian regime":** Interviewed in the documentary *Chicago Boys*, directed by Carola Fuentes and Rafael Valdeavellano (Icarus Films, 2015).

142 **The result was hundreds of civilian deaths and injuries:** Naomi Klein, *The Shock Doctrine: The Rise of Disaster Capitalism* (New York: Metropolitan Books, 2007), 222–31.

142 ***The Economist* had no reservations:** "Yeltsin Regrets," *Economist*, October 9, 1993, 15ff; also in Mattei, *The Capital Order*, 302.

143 **a small group of citizens appropriated:** Branko Milanović, *Income, Inequality, and Poverty During the Transition from Planned to Market Economy*, World Bank Regional and Sectoral Studies (Washington, DC: World Bank Group, 1998), 68. For information on suicides and addiction, see Klein, *The Shock Doctrine*, 237–38.

143 **The impact of these "Harvard Boys":** On the "Harvard Boys," see Klein, *The Shock Doctrine*, 224; and Janine R. Wedel, "The Harvard Boys Do Russia," *The Nation*, May 14, 1998, https://www.thenation.com/article/world/harvard-boys-do-russia/.

145 **Italian Communist Party and the British Labour Party:** On the austerity policies of the Italian Communist Party after the historic compromise, see M. J. Sodaro, "The Italian Communists and the Politics of Austerity," *Studies in Comparative Communism* 13, nos. 2/3 (1980): 220–49. On Britain, see Aaron Major, *Architects of Austerity: International Finance and the Politics of Growth* (Stanford University Press, 2014).

145 **"What is really striking about these political leaders":** Ralph Miliband, *The State in Capitalist Society* (London: Weidenfeld and Nicolson, 1969), 69–72.

146 **takes on a specific role:** For a good discussion on the specific form of the capitalist state, see Michael Heinrich, "State and Capital," chap. 11 in *An Introduction to the Three Volumes of Karl Marx's Capital*, trans. Alexander Locascio (New York: Monthly Review Press, 2004), 212.

146 **"Given their view of that system":** Miliband, *The State in Capitalist Society*, 75.

147 **He expressed this view at the Brussels conference:** League of Nations, *Proceedings of the Brussels International Financial Conference, 1920*, vol. 2 of 5, *Statistical Memoranda on Currency*,

Public Finance, and Trade (London: Harrison and Sons, 1920–1921), 109.
147 **"Lack of fiscal discipline is almost exclusively found":** Vittorio Grilli et al., "Political and Monetary Institutions and Public Financial Policies in the Industrial Countries," *Economic Policy* 6, no. 13 (1991): 342–92, particularly 359, https://doi.org/10.2307/1344630.
149 **The solution was to legitimize central banks:** Resolution III, Commission on Currency and Exchange, Brussels 1920, *Report of the Second Commission [Finance], Resolution I*, vol. 1, no 18, in Charles Gordon and Edouard Montpetit, *The Genoa Conference for the Economic and Financial Reconstruction of Europe: Joint Report of the Canadian Delegates* (Ottawa: F. A. Acland, 1922), 68.
149 **The influential British Treasury economist:** Ralph G. Hawtrey, "Currency and Public Administration," *Public Administration* 3, no. 3 (1925): 232–45, 243.
149 **Scientific articles laud the "social desirability":** Alberto Alesina and Lawrence H. Summers, "Central Bank Independence and Macroeconomic Performance: Some Comparative Evidence," *Journal of Money, Credit and Banking* 25, no. 2 (1993): 151–62, 151.
149 **It "explicitly forbids" the bank's board:** Article 7 in Alberto Alesina and Vittorio Grilli, "The European Central Bank: A New Instrument of Monetary Policy?," *International Economic Review* 32, no. 1 (1991): 13–27.
150 **This autonomy was reinforced:** On the Fed's rising independence and its chokehold over monetary policies, see Stephen Maher and Scott Aquanno, *The Fall and Rise of American Finance: From J. P. Morgan to BlackRock* (London: Verso Books, 2024), especially 63–70 and 125–129; and Herbert Stein, *The Fiscal Revolution in America: Policy in Pursuit of Reality*, 2nd rev. ed. (Washington, DC: AEI Press, 1996). About the post-WWII period, Maher and Aquanno write:
>The power of the Fed to manage the economy was considered just as sacred as, and even less partisan than, the Supreme Court's authority to interpret the law. With the crucial questions of economic policy decided in venues that were largely outside of public view and beyond the reach of elections—and which thereby embodied 'the continuity of the state' regardless of electoral outcomes—politics increasingly focused on cultural and civil rights issues *within* the structure of corporate capitalism. (133)

150 **At that time, the Fed claimed:** For the new role of the Fed as dealer of last resort in the 2020s, see Maher and Aquanno, *The Fall and Rise of American Finance*, 197–205.
150 **The Fed purchased corporate debt:** On the COVID-19 programs, see Maher and Aquanno, *The Fall and Rise of American Finance*, 200–201; and Mark Watson III, "How Big Corporations Scored Coronavirus Relief and Small Businesses Lost Out," *San Antonio Report*, July 8,

NOTES

2020, https://sanantonioreport.org/how-big-corporations-scored-coronavirus-relief-and-small-businesses-lost-out/.

151 **valued at approximately $4.6 billion:** Eshita Bhargava, "Mukesh Ambani and Anant Ambani's $4.6 Billion 27-Storey Skyscraper Home Has a Snow Room, Spa, Ice-Cream Parlor, and More," *Financial Express*, April 19, 2023, https://www.financialexpress.com/life/lifestyle-mukesh-ambanis-4-6-billion-27-story-skyscraper-home-has-a-snow-room-spa-ice-cream-parlor-and-more-2891686/.

152 **more than 820 million people:** Hanna Duggal and Marium Ali, "Why Do More Than 800 Million People Live in Hunger?," Al Jazeera, May 28, 2023, https://www.aljazeera.com/news/2023/5/28/why-is-global-hunger-on-the-rise-2.

152 **2,600 billionaires add $2.7 billion:** "Richest 1% Bag Nearly Twice as Much Wealth as the Rest of the World Put Together over the Past Two Years," Oxfam International, press release, January 16, 2023, https://www.oxfam.org/en/press-releases/richest-1-bag-nearly-twice-much-wealth-rest-world-put-together-over-past-two-years.

153 **The genocide in Gaza and the destruction of our ecosystem:** For a fundamental piece looking at the parallels and complementary stories of Palestine and the climate, see Andreas Malm, "The Destruction of Palestine Is the Destruction of the Earth," Verso Books, blog post, April 8, 2024, https://www.versobooks.com/blogs/news/the-destruction-of-palestine-is-the-destruction-of-the-earth; and Wim Carton and Andreas Malm, *Overshoot: How the World Surrendered to Climate Breakdown* (London: Verso Books, 2023).

153 **the revenue of the world's top one hundred arms companies:** "World's Top Arms Producers See Revenues Rise on the Back of Wars and Regional Tensions," Stockholm International Peace Research Institute, press release, December 2, 2024, https://www.sipri.org/media/press-release/2024/worlds-top-arms-producers-see-revenues-rise-back-wars-and-regional-tensions.

153 **In her extraordinary June 2025 UN report:** UN Human Rights Council, *From Economy of Occupation to Economy of Genocide: Report of the Special Rapporteur on the Situation of Human Rights in the Palestinian Territories Occupied Since 1967*, Francesca Albanese, A/HRC/59/23 (June 30, 2025), https://www.un.org/unispal/document/a-hrc-59-23-from-economy-of-occupation-to-economy-of-genocide-report-special-rapporteur-francesca-albanese-palestine-2025/.

154 **A 1959 cost-benefit analysis of defense spending:** Tim Barker, "Cold War Capitalism: The Political Economy of American Military Spending, 1947–1990" (doctoral dissertation, Harvard University, 2022). This meticulous study on military Keynesianism reveals how the economic boom during the so-called golden age of capitalism was driven primarily by militarism.

154 **Although the richest 10 percent:** Kohei Saito, *Slow Down: The Degrowth Manifesto* (New York: Astra, 2024), 52.
154 **These retorts propose false alternatives:** Even if Chinese central planning is a very different reality from our anarchic market dynamics, and the Chinese Communist Party has much more control over economic interests, 80 percent of the Chinese workforce is employed in the private sector as wage workers, and while Soviet Russia did abolish private means of production, workers there were still working for a wage and were not in control of their laboring activity. On China, see Ying Chen, "Capitalism, Socialism and Ideology in China: An Alternative Historical Materialist Analysis," *Science and Society* 85, no. 3 (2021): 385–91; and Minqi Li, *The Rise of China and the Demise of the Capitalist World Economy* (New York: Monthly Review Press, 2009). On Russia, see Alec Nove, *An Economic History of the USSR: 1917–1991* (London: Penguin, 1992).
155 **"Revolutionary dreams":** Robin D. G. Kelley, *Freedom Dreams: The Black Radical Imagination* (Boston: Beacon Press, 2002), 8.
158 **At the same time, the movement:** One percent of large landowners control 90 percent of agricultural land—and industrial agriculture has led to even greater concentration of rural property ownership. See Maria Luisa Mendonça, "Farmland Assets," *Phenomenal World*, May 28, 2022, https://www.phenomenalworld.org/analysis/farmland-assets/.
159 **decisions that shape their lives:** Jacob Masterson, "Uma Luta de Todos! The Landless Rural Workers Movement in Brazil: From Land to Democracy (1985–2023)" (undergraduate thesis, Ohio State University, 2024), https://kb.osu.edu/server/api/core/bitstreams/5daa595f-3086-49e5-a351-77cb2a540dcb/content.
159 **biggest producer of organic rice in Latin America:** Rodrigo Chagas and Pedro Stropasolas, "Organic Rice from MST Crops: Agroecology Can Produce on a Large Scale and Oppose Agribusiness," *Brasil de Fato*, republished on MST website, April 17, 2023, https://mst.org.br/2023/04/17/organic-rice-from-mst-crops-agroecology-can-produce-on-a-large-scale-and-oppose-agribusiness/.
160 **The rural front for a postcapitalist world:** On the history of the MTST, see Guilherme Simões, Marcos Campos, and Rud Rafael, *MTST: 20 Anos de História; Luta, Organização e Esperança nas Periferias do Brasil* (São Paulo: Editora Fundação Perseu Abramo, 2017).
160 **"People are living a hell in the big cities":** Nilton Viana, "The Meaning and Prospects of the Street Mobilizations: An Interview with João Pedro Stedile," *Brasil de Fato*, republished on Friends of the MST website, June 25, 2013, https://mstbrazil.org/news/meaning-prospects-street-mobilizations-interview-jo%C3%A3o-pedro-stedile.
160 **Its research center:** Marisol León, "Learning to Fight: The MST's Escola Nacional and Its Pedagogy of Resistance" (independent study

project, School for International Training, Spring 2006), 393, https://digitalcollections.sit.edu/isp_collection/393.

160 **Meanwhile, workers operate:** *The Take*, written by Naomi Klein, directed by Avi Lewis (First Run Features / Icarus Films, 2004); F. C. Henriques, *Autogestão em Empresas Recuperadas por Trabalhadores: Brasil e Argentina* [Self-management in companies recovered by workers: Brazil and Argentina], vol. 4, Série Tecnologia Social (Santos: Insular, 2013); Manoel Santana dos Santos and Carlos Mário Bittar, *Dialética da autogestão em empresas recuperadas por trabalhadores no Brasil* [Dialectics of self-management in companies recovered by workers in Brazil] (São Paulo: Annablume, 2015); Bruno T. Rabelo, *Um Horizonte de Lutas para a Autogestão: O Trabalho Organizado por Plataforma Digital* [A horizon of struggles for self-management: Work organized by digital platforms] (São Paulo: Lutas Anticapital, 2024).

161 **9.2 million indirect jobs:** "Sheinbaum Launches Program to Construct 1 Million Homes," *Mexico Business News*, November 20, 2023, https://mexicobusiness.news/infrastructure/news/sheinbaum-launches-program-construct-1-million-homes.

161 **ambitiously about their economic rights:** Luke Taylor, "'Living Proof That You Can Spend Money on the Poor': Utopia Comes to Mexico City," *The Guardian*, December 27, 2024, https://www.theguardian.com/global-development/2024/dec/27/mexico-city-utopias-project-mayor.

162 **driving a new political movement:** "People Have Spoken: African Youth and Kenyan Finance Bill Protests," Wilson Center, September 3, 2024, https://www.wilsoncenter.org/blog-post/people-have-spoken-african-youth-and-kenyan-finance-bill-protests; Andres Schipani, "How a 'Bunch of Nobodies' Left Kenya's Political Class Running Scared," *Financial Times*, July 26, 2024, https://www.ft.com/content/43631faf-16bc-487e-8e9a-b3e23c4b8a72; "Kenya's Ruto Faces IMF, Protests, and Tax Bill," *Foreign Policy*, July 3, 2024, https://foreignpolicy.com/2024/07/03/kenya-william-ruto-imf-protests-tax-bill/; "Africa's Cost-of-Living Protests Reach Nigeria," *Wall Street Journal*, July 9, 2024, https://www.wsj.com/world/africa/africas-cost-of-living-protests-reach-nigeria-d0b507f1.

162 **"From Citizen to Producer":** Zino Zini, "Da cittadino a produttore," *L'Ordine Nuovo* 1, no. 38 (February 21, 1920): 301–2.

INDEX

Note: Pages after 166 refer to notes.

absolute surplus value, 43–44
abstract labour, 175
accumulation
   about, 37–38
   by dispossession, 175
   employment and, 186–87
   environmental issues and, 174
   militarism and, 153
   technology and, 96
   See also capitalism overview; profit
acquisitions, 49–50
Addison, Christopher, 72
Africa, 98, 115–17, 118–19, 120, 135, 161–62
agency, 76–77
Agnelli, Giovanni, 3
agriculture, 96, 200
aid. See loans
Albanese, Francesca, 153
Alesina, Alberto, 88–89
algorithms, 46–47, 51
Allende, Salvador, 141
alternatives to capitalism, 15. See also transformation
Amazon
   acquisitions, 50
   competition, 52–53
   Palestine and, 153
   tax breaks, 98–99
   technology and, 46, 177
   unions and, 47, 101, 105
Amazon Web Services, 51
Amin, Samir, 115–16
Antilia, 151
antisemitism, 17
Apple, 43, 51
Aquanno, Scott, 11, 179, 180, 198
Ardagna, Silvia, 88–89
Argentina, 118

INDEX

arms industry, 153
artificial intelligence (AI), 96–97
asset management firms, 52
AT&T, 61
austerity
   about, 57–59, 63, 90, 91
   in Argentina, 90–91
   challenging, 156
   in Chile, 141–42
   competition and, 113–14
   crisis of capitalism and, 66
   defined, 57, 58
   in Europe, 2–3, 150–51
   as expensive, 64
   fascism and, 5, 77, 80–81
   goal of, 59
   in India, 89
   interest rates and, 62–63, 135, 137
   in Israel, 132
   in Italy, 5, 77, 80–81, 113–14
   in Kenya, 162
   life expectancy and, 65–66
   loans and, 117–19
   as objective reality, 78
   in Palestine, 126–27
   political leanings and, 145
   public employees and, 89
   pure economics and, 82–83
   in Russia, 142–43
   in Sri Lanka, 137
   state and, 61–62
   taxes and, 60–61, 64
   unemployment and, 137
   See also coercion
authoritarian governments, 141–43. *See also* fascism; Mussolini, Benito
auto industry, 49, 104–5
autonomy, 119

banks, 11, 51–52, 136, 149–50, 186
basic income, 88, 148
begging, 27
Behar, Amitabh, 151
Beneduce, Alberto, 2–3
Bezos, Jeff, 47. *See also* Amazon
Bhattacharya, Tithi, 41
Bidenomics, 58
billionaires, 9, 36, 115
Black people, 34. *See also* racialized people; racism
BlackRock, 52, 59, 153
blame, 90
Blanchard, Olivier, 111
Blockbuster, 43
Bolshevism, 79
borrowing money, 117
Brand, Robert H., 1–2
Brazil, 120, 136, 156–57
Britain, 122–23
Brugada, Clara, 161

Cannibal Capitalism (Fraser), 172, 188
capital, 86–87
Capital (Marx), 174
capital gains, 64
Capitalism (Shaikh), 180
Capitalism, Alone (Milanović), 173–74
capitalism overview
   capitalism as precise, 61, 65, 152
   contradictions, 178, 186–87
   crisis of capitalism, 66, 67, 70–77, 140 (*see also* inflation; strikes)
   defined, 22
   defined by De' Stefani, 85
   democracy and, 144, 147
   finance vs. industrial capital, 179
   freedom in, 27–28
   full employment, 93, 100, 186, 187
   golden age of, 44
   history of, 22–27
   inequities, 9
   internalization and, 145–47
   naturalization of capitalism, 8, 9–10, 27

poverty relationship, 33
the state and, 144–46
capital order, 9–10, 19, 36–37, 55, 57
carbon dioxide, 154
central banks, 11, 136, 149–50, 186
centralization, 51–52
CEOs, 35
Chalmers, Robert, 2
Chang, Ha-Joon, 116
chapter overviews, 15–16
ChatGPT, 96–97
checkpoints, 121, 129, 132
Chen, Jing, 115, 175
Cherokee people, 24
Chicago Boys, 141–42
Chicago School of Economics, 94, 186
children, 20, 21, 131, 151
Chile, 141–42
China, 154, 200
choices, 114
class
 about, 22, 31–34
 in Brazil, 136
 economic studies and, 10
 in Israel, 134–35
 in Palestine, 129, 135
 racism and, 34
 in South Africa, 135
 in Sri Lanka, 136–38
 wage labor and, 28
 See also wage labor
class conflict, 10, 32, 78, 91. *See also* crisis of capitalism; occupations; strikes
"classlessness," 78
climate disasters, 120
climate refugees, 138
cloud services, 51, 179
coercion, 29, 66, 89
Coin, Francesca, 99
collectives, 24, 155–57, 160–61
colonization, 24
commodities, 19–20, 42

communes, 156–57
communism, 80, 154, 200
community, 73, 155
competition
 about, 42–43
 acquisitions, 49
 austerity and, 113–14
 centralization and, 51–52
 drive of, 52–53
 exploitation and, 43–47
 failure and, 43
 financialization and, 179, 180
 as inherent to capitalism, 55
 neoclassical economics' views, 53–54
 vs. protectionism, 116–17
 quantity theory of, 179–80
 rhetoric about, 53
 technology and, 46–48, 95–97
 unemployment and, 95–97, 101–2, 103
 unrealism of, 180
 See also profit
Comuna da Terra Irma Alberta, 156–59
concrete labor, 175
consumption, 184–85
Cook, Tim, 35
Cooperation Tulsa, 155
councils, 4, 74–76, 155
COVID-19 pandemic, 6, 103–4, 168
crisis of capitalism, 66, 67, 70–77, 140. *See also* inflation; strikes
cybersecurity, 132
cyclical accumulation, 187

debt, 138, 150
deficits, 182
democracy, 12, 109, 144, 147–48
dependency, 117–19
depoliticization, 7
deregulation, 89
De' Stefani, Alberto, 79–80, 81–83, 85, 140
developing countries, 115

INDEX

Dharavi, 152
digital platforms, 51, 179
discipline, 6, 63. *See also* austerity
discount rates, 184–85
Domash, Alex, 111
Dowbor, Ladislau, 136
Draghi, Mario, 113
drones, 132

economic freedom, 163
"Economic Possibilities for Our Grandchildren" (Keynes), 187
economics professors, 78–79
economists
   about, 6–7, 11
   class conflict and, 10
   human beings and, 84
   idealizing capitalism, 78
   masking vs. explaining, 8–9
   Mattei as, 16
   unemployment as data set, 93
   See also individual economists
economy as political, 13–14
education, 73
eight-hour days, 44
Einaudi, Luigi, 4, 80–81, 85, 88
elections. *See* voting
electricity, 128
Elizabeth I (queen of England), 27
employment, 5–6. *See also* full employment; unemployment
end of history, 22–23
Engels, Friedrich, 35
environmental issues, 120, 154, 174
Espinoza, Juan, 46
European Central Bank, 149
exchange value, 20
executions, 27
exploitation
   about, 38–42
   algorithms, 46–47
   competition and, 43–47
   financialization and, 179
   by governments, 69–70

   Keynes' ideas, 187
   profit and, 38–42, 178
   safety, 50–51
   value and, 50
   wages and, 45–46, 49
expropriation, 24, 102

factory councils, 4, 74–76, 155
factory occupations, 3
The Fall and Rise of American Finance (Aquanno and Maher), 179, 180
fascism
   austerity and, 90
   capitalism and, 79–82
   economic experts in Italy, 4–5
   liberalism and, 140–41
   resistance in Italy, 17–18
   worker power and, 75
   See also Mussolini, Benito
Federal Reserve, 5, 149–50, 198
feudalism, 24–25, 29
Fiat, 3, 75
FIFA World Cup, 102
finance capital, 179
financialization, 179, 180
financial speculation, 97
First Intifada, 130
fiscal austerity, 58, 60, 62, 89. *See also* austerity
Foley, Duncan, 111–12
food, 21. *See also* hunger
food assistance, 64
food sovereignty, 158
Ford factory model, 44–45
Forum for Humane Economics (FREE), 155
Foxconn, 51
Frank, Andre Gunder, 115–16
Fraser, Nancy, 102, 172, 188
freedom, 27–29, 163
Freedom Flotilla, 162
free markets, 155
Fukuyama, Francis, 22–23
full employment, 93, 100, 186, 187

INDEX

Galbraith, James Kenneth, 94–95, 115, 175
Gaza. *See* Palestine
Geddes, Eric, 72
Geller, Ilya, 46
genocide, 132–33. *See also* Palestine
Ghana, 116–17, 118
Giolitti, Giovanni, 75
Global North
  about, 115
  amount extracted from Global South, 119
  dependency on, 117–18
  Israel and, 122–23
  underdevelopment and, 116, 117
  See also Global South; Israel; migrant workers; *individual countries*
Global South
  amount extracted, 119
  central bank models, 149
  debt problems, 138
  dependency and, 117–19
  environmental issues, 120, 154
  foreign capital and, 119
  inequity in, 151–52
  See also Global North; migrant workers; Palestine; *individual countries*
Goodwin, Richard, 187
Google, 49–50
Gramsci, Antonio, 4, 73, 75–76, 77, 154
Great Britain, 72–74
Great Resignation, 7, 8, 168
The Great War, 2, 67–70
greed, 42
Grilli, Vittorio, 147
Gross domestic product (GDP)
  about, 36, 174
  in Brazil, 136
  in Israel, 121
  in Palestine, 195
  workers and, 97–98

growing wealth. *See* accumulation; profit
Gurner, Tim, 6

Harvey, David, 50, 175
Hawtrey, Ralph, 149
healthcare, 65
Henry VIII (king of England), 27
Hever, Shir, 192–93
hierarchy, 11
high capital/high labor, 174
Hitler, Adolf, 90
homelessness, 20, 21, 45. *See also* poverty
Homeless Workers' Movement (MTST), 160
hospitality, 105
housing, 161
hunger, 21, 64, 120, 137, 152. *See also* poverty

immigration, 102
impatience, 184–85
imports/exports, 117
Indian Removal Act, 24
Indigenous Peoples, 24, 30
industrial austerity, 63, 89. *See also* austerity
industrial capital, 179
inflation
  in 1919, 7
  about, 7, 106–7, 111–12
  democracy and, 109
  as moral deficiency, 4–5
  NAIRU, 107–8
  profit and, 109–10
  suffering for, 5
  unemployment and, 106–8, 109–11
  and unionization, 8
interest rates
  austerity and, 62–63, 135, 137
  foreign capital and, 119
  on loans, 135
  raising, 5–6, 62–63, 111

interest rates (*cont.*)
  recessions and, 13
  unemployment and, 111
international economics
  conferences, 1–3, 77–78, 79
International Monetary Fund
  (IMF), 117–18, 137, 142
investors, 11–12
invisible hand, 67
iPhones, 43
Israel, 58, 120–35, 194. *See also*
  Palestine
Italy
  capital trap in, 113–14
  economic experts in, 4–5
  factory occupations, 3
  Red Biennium, 71–75
  self-governance, 3–4, 74, 183
  tomato industry, 102
  unemployment, 99–100
  workers as soldiers, 69
  See also Mussolini, Benito

jobs. *See* employment; full
  employment; unemployment
J. P. Morgan and Co., 139
JPMorganChase, 51

Kalecki, Michał, 100, 187
Kelley, Robin, 155
Kenya, 161–62
Keynes, John Maynard
  on Chicago School, 94
  employment and, 100
  on inflation, 4, 7
  markets and resources, 186
  utopianism, 187

labor, defined, 175
Labor Action Tracker, 189
labor power, 39–40, 175
land, 25–27, 29–30, 183, 200. *See also* Palestine
Landless Workers' Movement
  (MST), 158–59

La Via Campesina, 159
League of Nations, 2
Leonardo, 153
liberalism, 81, 90, 140–41, 143–45, 148
life expectancy, 65–66
living wages, 45
loans, 117–19, 135
Lockheed Martin, 59
Loewenstein, Antony, 138
logistics. *See* Amazon
L'Ordine nuovo (magazine), 73, 75, 77
Luders, Rolf, 142
Lula, 120

Maastricht Treaty, 150–51
Maher, Stephen, 11, 179, 180, 198
market history, 23
Marx, Karl/Marxism
  about, 10
  on bourgeoisie, 47–48
  on contradictions, 186–87
  Einaudi on, 85
  on environmental issues, 174
  on expropriation, 30–31
  on labor and labor power, 175
  on unemployment, 95, 101
math, 180. *See also* pure economics
Mattei, Camillo, 17
Mattei, Gianfranco, 18
Mattei, Teresa, 17–18
McNally, David, 171
meatpacking industry, 102–3
Medicaid, 65
medical care, 33
Mekorot, 121, 127–28
Meloni, Giorgia, 88, 113
merit as hierarchy, 11
meritocracy, 86
Mexico, 161
Microsoft Azure, 51
middle class, 9, 31–32. *See also* class
migrant workers, 102, 130, 138
Milanović, Branko, 173–74
Milei, Javier, 15, 89, 90–91

Miliband, Ralph, 144–45, 146
military, 58, 59, 132–33, 153–54
Minalba, 157
minimum wage, 102–3
Modi, Narendra, 89
monetary austerity, 62. *See also* austerity
monitoring technologies, 46–47
monopolies, 110
moral deficiency, 4–5
morality, 38
Morgan, Jack, Jr., 139
Movimento dos Trabalhadores Rurais Sem Terra (MST), 158–60
Movimento dos Trabalhadores Sem Teto (MTST), 160
multinationals, 118
Musk, Elon, 15
Mussolini, Benito
   accumulation and, 113
   austerity and, 5, 77, 80–81
   Bank of England and, 139
   economic experts and, 78–82
   liberalism and, 140
   Pantaleoni and, 147
   worker power and, 75

Nakba, 123
nationalization, 68–69
Native Americans, 24
Nazi Germany, 90
Nenni, Pietro, 71
neoclassical economics
   about, 95
   competition, 53–54, 180
   impatience and, 184–85
   inflation, 106
   objectivity, 10–11
   See also pure economics
neoclassical paradigm, 79
neoliberalism, 179
Netanyahu, Benjamin, 132
Netflix, 43
New Deal, 29
New History of Capitalism, 171

New Smithian, 170–71
non-accelerating inflation rate of unemployment (NAIRU), 107
Norman, Montagu, 139

occupations (by workers), 3, 74, 183. *See also* strikes
occupied land. *See* Palestine
oligarchs, 143
Ömer, Özlem, 32–33
"One Big Beautiful Bill," 64
one percent, 60, 152
The Origin of Capitalism (Wood), 170

Palestine, 58, 120–35, 153, 162, 192–95
The Palestine Laboratory (Loewenstein), 132
Palestinian Authority, 124–25, 193
Pantaleoni, Maffeo, 4–5, 79, 82–83, 86, 87, 147
pauperism, 27
Pedro Stedile, Joao, 160
Phillips curve, 106–7
Pietravalle, Michele, 72
Pinochet, Augusto, 141–42
political, as term, 14
"Political Aspects of Full Employment" (Kalecki), 187
political economy, 11
The Political Economy of Israel's Occupation (Hever), 192–93
political freedom, 163
poverty
   children in, 9, 58, 151
   choice and, 114
   globally, 12
   in Global South, 33
   history of, 27
   income loss and, 182
   in India, 151–52
   as inherent to capitalism, 33
   in Israel, 134–35
   as laziness, 87–88
   in New York City, 20

poverty (*cont.*)
   United States in 1962, 33
   vs. wealth, 26–27, 36, 60, 65–66, 116, 151–52
   working poor, 45
   See also homelessness; wealth
Powell, Jerome, 5
power imbalances, 111
praxis, 75
precarity, 33, 89, 102–3
Price, Richard, 26
prices, 50, 108, 109–10. *See also* competition; inflation
Principles of Pure Economics (Panteleoni), 79
Prison Notebooks (Gramsci), 75
private ownership/privatization
   in capitalism, 22, 25–26
   IMF and, 118
   land, 25–27, 30
   Palestinian land, 122
   as preparing workers, 88
   replacing, 3
   in Russia, 143
   shareholders and, 119
   water, 91
production costs, 178
production theory, 175
productivity, 44–45, 46–47, 67–68
profit
   about, 21, 37–38
   exploitation and, 38–42, 178
   Ford factory model and, 44–45
   inflation and, 109–10
   iPhones, 43
   limits to, 69, 108–9
   as modern concept, 22
   productivity and, 48
   as surplus value, 40–41
   unemployment and, 107
   unpaid wage labor and, 41–42
   well-being and, 9
   See also accumulation; competition
protectionism, 116–17

protest, 161–62. *See also* transformation
public employees, 64, 88, 126
public investment, 160–61
public works programs, 29
pure economics, 11, 82–86, 94

quantity theory of competition, 179–80

racialized people, 33, 103, 175. *See also* immigration
racism, 34, 188
Rana Plaza textile factory, 50–51
real wages, 45
recessions, 13, 63
reconstructionists, 71–72
Red Biennium, 71–75
redistribution, 29, 148, 150
reforms, 156
refugees, 138
Reich, Robert, 110
relative surplus value, 44–45
rents (competition), 53
repression, 187
revolution, 154–55
Ricardo, David, 10, 31
Ricci, Umberto, 80, 82–83, 84–85, 86
Rostow, Walt, 114–15
RTX Corporation, 153
Russell, Catherine, 131
Russia, 142–43, 154, 200

safety, 50–51, 102–3
Saito, Kohei, 120
self-management, 160. *See also* occupations
Shaikh, Anwar, 53–54, 180
shareholders, 35, 119
Sheinbaum, Claudia, 161
Shell Global, 98
shelter, 20
Shikaki, Ibrahim, 121, 129
Silva, Luiz Inacio Lula da, 120

INDEX

Smith, Adam, 10, 31
social services, 59, 72–73, 118. *See also* welfare
solidarity kitchens, 160
South Africa, 135
Sri Lanka, 136–38
stabilization, 63–64
"The Stages of Economic Growth" (Rostow), 114–15
the state, 58, 144–46, 190
The State in Capitalist Society (Miliband), 144–45, 146
State Street, 52
stocks, 97, 153
strikes
  in 1919, 74
  full employment and, 187
  increasing, 105
  India, 30
  Labor Action Tracker, 189
  logistics and hospitality, 105
  as outlawed, 113
  in Palestine, 130
  UAW, 104–6
  writers, 105
  See also occupations
students, 155
suffering, 2, 5–6
suicide, 51
Summers, Lawrence H., 109, 111
surplus value, 40–41, 43–45, 178
surveillance, 131–33
sweatshops, 50

taxes
  Amazon and, 99
  austerity and, 60–61, 64
  to corporations, 108–9
  in Palestine, 122, 124, 125
Taylor, Lance, 32–33
technocracy, 84
Technofeudalism (Varoufakis), 179
technology, 46, 47, 95–97, 186–87
textile factories, 50–51
theft, 175

Thunberg, Greta, 162
Togliatti, Palmiro, 73
Trail of Tears, 24
transformation, 155–63
Trump, Donald, 15, 61, 64

U-6, 188
unemployment
  in 2020s, 103–4, 111
  about, 93–94, 186
  austerity and, 137
  competition and, 95–97, 101–2, 103
  as data set, 93
  as discipline device, 6, 63
  Great Resignation, 168
  inflation and, 106–8, 109–11
  in Italy, 99–100
  NAIRU, 107–8
  as necessary to capitalism, 98, 101, 111
  official vs. reality, 188
  in Palestine, 130
  as paradox in capitalism, 95, 100
  profit and, 107
  structural biases towards, 95
  unionization and, 101
  wages and, 106–7
  worker dissatisfaction and, 99, 168
  See also full employment
unions, 47, 101, 104, 113
United Auto Workers (UAW), 104–6
United Kingdom, 72–74
universal basic income, 29
unpaid labor, 41–42
UPS, 105
use value, 20

Vagabonds Act (England), 27
value
  exchange value, 20
  exploitation and, 50
  labor and, 175
  surplus value, 40–41, 43–45, 178

Vanguard, 52, 153
Varoufakis, Yanis, 46, 179
Volcker, Paul, 63
voting, 14, 144, 145, 162–63, 198

wage labor
   about, 22, 28
   accumulation and, 186–87
   Amazon consultants and, 177
   capital order and, 36–37
   commodities and, 28
   freedom and, 27–29
   history of, 26–27
   labor power, 39–40
   living wages, 45
   Marx on, 30–31
   racism and, 34
   real wages, 45
   as redundant workers, 95, 96, 98
   technology and, 96–97
   universal basic income and, 29
   unpaid labor, 41–42
   wage freezes, 70
   wages and unemployment, 106–7
   wages and working-class reproduction, 176
   wages at Walmart, 49, 100
   workers as unhappy, 99, 168
   See also exploitation; unemployment
wage-price spiral. *See* inflation
Walmart, 48–49, 100
Walt Disney Company, 60
water, 127–28
wealth
   GDP and, 36
   Global North as, 115
   growing wealth, 9, 35–36
   inheritance tax and, 61, 64
   merit and, 11
   in New York City, 20
   as one percent, 33, 34
   vs. poverty, 26–27, 36, 60, 65–66, 116, 151–52
   racism and, 34
   taxes and, 65
   See also class; class conflict; Global North; poverty
welfare, 29, 87–88. *See also* social services
western countries. *See* Global North; wealth
Wolff, Richard D., 109
Wood, Ellen Meiksins, 170–71
workday hours, 43–44, 187
workers as soldiers, 69
workers' councils, 4, 74–76, 155
working class. *See* class; class conflict; wage labor
working poor, 45, 88
World Bank, 117
World War I, 2, 67–70
writers, 105

Yellen, Janet, 5–6, 62
Yeltsin, Boris, 142–43

Zini, Zino, 162–63